I love how this book has laid out the possible steps along a pathway to a more fully formed discipleship and experience with God.

—**Bishop Robert D. Farr**, Missouri Annual Conference of
The United Methodist Church

Roger Ross has the gift of speaking directly into the human heart. In this book, he names what many believers sense, there must be "more." Roger not only explores the substance of the ever illusive "more;" he helps us discover it for ourselves.

—**Shane L. Bishop**, Sr. Pastor, Christ Church, Fairview Heights, Illinois.
Author of *That's Good News*, *The PING Life* and the *Trail Guide* series

Roger Ross knows that experiencing an abundant life in Jesus involves a collaborative process between God and us. God's Spirit draws us to himself, then we play our part by positioning ourselves to receive his grace and life. Let Roger guide you along the ancient-yet-modern pathways that move us from passive waiting to joyful receiving of all God has for us. Step one: read this book.

-**Rev. Dr. Steve Cordle**, Director of Church Multiplication for the
Global Methodist Church and Executive Director of The River Network International

Roger Ross has a pastor's heart, wanting to see people in the church deepen their relationship with Jesus Christ so that they might know the full joy of living in God's grace. This book provides a generous pathway for persons to move their relationship with God through Jesus to more profound dimensions. It offers practical and practicable ideas, rooted in the Scriptures and grounded in experience, for anyone wanting to live more fully into their faith. I commend this insightful guide to becoming a deeply devoted disciple.

—**Bishop David A. Bard**, Bishop for the Illinois Great Rivers and
Michigan Conferences of The United Methodist Church

Roger Ross' *Kinda Christian* is a gift to pastors and lay leaders who long to become deeply devoted disciples—and to lead their churches there, too. Clear, practical, and Spirit-anchored, it lays out a G6 pathway (Glory, Grace, Group, Growth, Giftedness, Generosity) that any congregation can adopt and adapt. Leaders will find both a compelling vision for personal transformation and a step-by-step process for building a local discipleship pathway that forms people who love God, launch authentic community, and unleash compassion. If you're ready to move your church from "curious" to "serious" about Jesus, this book will show you how—and give you the tools to begin now.

—**Rev. Dr. Bener Baysa Agtarap** is Executive Director of Path 1 and Director of Connectional Mobilization at Discipleship Ministries of The United Methodist Church.

Roger Ross raises vital questions that most pastors and churches overlook amid the whirlwind of ministry—what is a disciple and how are they made? With great care, Ross connects with both church insiders and outsiders, drawing each into a more committed relationship with Jesus and passion for his mission. As a local church pastor, I feel confident sharing this easy read with a spiritual seeker curious about faith as well as leaders who desire to clarify their own church's discipleship pathway. *Kinda Christian* is a great tool for ministry!

-**Rev. Dr. Andy Adams**, Senior Pastor of Troy Methodist Church, Troy, Illinois

The Christian life does not simply start and stop at becoming a disciple, but instead with *making* deeply devoted disciples. Ross' *Kinda Christian* taps into the longing of following Jesus above and beyond intellectual assent and, instead, committing one's whole self to the journey of becoming more like Jesus. The time of cultural Christianity has passed us by and is unfulfilling in comparison to the abundant life Jesus has for his followers.

-**Rev. Dr. Rosario "Roz" Picardo**, church planter, author, professor and coach

For nearly two decades, I've watched Roger Ross live the message he writes about here. This book captures his deep love for Jesus and his heart to see others move from empty ritual to authentic relationship. With vivid stories and clear steps, Roger guides us into a grace-filled journey of true discipleship. Every pastor, leader, and follower of Christ will be enriched by these pages.

-**Rev. Ricky Spindler**, Lead Pastor, Stone Creek Church, Urbana, Illinois

Kinda Christian, by Rev. Roger Ross, is more than a book, it is a discipleship journey blessing. I wholeheartedly commend it to every follower of Jesus. May it renew your journey, replenish your spirit, and be a reminder that discipleship is a holy, sacred, and active journey.

-**Rev. Dr. Susan Arnold**, Executive Director of Congregational Development & Connectional Ministries, Holston Conference, The United Methodist Church

Kinda Christian

Kinda Christian

FROM CURIOUS TO SERIOUS ABOUT JESUS

ROGER ROSS

 invite
PRESS

Plano, Texas

Contents

Introduction — Is There More?   xiii

Section One: Deeply Devoted Disciples

God Up Close   1

Grace Awakening   15

Life Together   32

Soul Food for the Long Run   52

Puzzling with God   71

Life Multiplied   87

Section Two: Disciples Who Make Disciples

Soul Sync   111

Jump in the River   122

Join The Revolution   133

Acknowledgments   137

Appendix A   139

About the Author   143

To Leanne
A deeply devoted, fiercely loyal, truly loving disciple of Jesus and the love of my life

Is There More?

Christianity, if false, is of no importance, and if true, of infinite importance. The only thing it cannot be is moderately important.

—*C. S. Lewis*

"They are just different names for the same thing."

That's what many people in Western culture would say when given a choice between identifying as a Christian or a disciple of Jesus.

Lauren would agree. At least, she would have as a young adult. But as her life unfolded, things changed. I first met Lauren while serving as a pastor at her parents' church. She lived in a different city and would occasionally come "home" to visit her mom and dad. Once or twice a year, she would attend church with them, and we would have a brief conversation after the service. Her life seemed full of work and friends and sounded carefree. I always enjoyed our talks but sensed there was something beneath her smile she kept carefully under wraps.

Off Guard

Four years later, I reconnected with Lauren and could see her life was radically different. Amazed by the transformation, I asked about her story. She was hesitant to say anything at first, but after praying, she shared some of her early journey. It caught me completely off guard.

> *If I were to characterize my life before following Jesus in one word, it would be "quitter." When I left home for college and found out that there*

were people who did not go to church on Sunday morning, I quit attending too. When school got hard in my 3rd year and I had more questions than answers about what I wanted to do with my life, I quit college and moved back home. I got a job and found a nice young man who wanted to marry me. It wasn't long before we found that being married was hard, and we both wanted out, so we quit.

When my marriage ended, I was humiliated by the pattern I was seeing in my life. I felt like a failure but didn't know what to do about it, so I quit a lot of things. I quit my job and moved to a new town, I quit seeing my friends, and I quit initiating contact with my family. I wanted to live my life in such a way that no one would know me too well—to keep people at a distance. That way, they wouldn't see how messed up my life was.

So, I spent my time hanging out in bars, drinking, and talking about surface level things. If anyone tried to get too close, they were gone. If they wanted to talk about anything other than the next fun thing we were doing, I wouldn't hear of it. If they (heaven forbid) needed me for support, I shut down.

I knew my life wasn't working, but I didn't know why.

Lauren's not alone. Like so many of us, she was trying to navigate a vast spiritual wilderness all by herself. As she shared her story, I felt her deep heartache and wondered if it could have been avoided. After all, she grew up in church.

Lauren and her family attended every Sunday. She participated in Sunday school and youth group regularly. When the time came, she went through confirmation class and became a member. Church was a huge part of her life. But it wasn't satisfying.

She remembers thinking, "I'm doing church. I know the routine, but it doesn't feel personal. Is there more?"

A Host of Pursuits

Let's pause there. Lauren's story represents millions of spiritual explorers on a journey of self-discovery. Like her, many of us have left home, cut ties with our past, and are determined to find ourselves in a host of pursuits our world defines as fun. Yet the longer we travel down this road, the more aimless our lives feel.

If someone had asked Lauren if she was a Christian at that time, she would have said yes without hesitation. She held certain beliefs about God and Jesus in her head. She attended church occasionally and still considered herself a member. Lauren certainly knew the broad outline of the Christian story, yet she felt lost, fearful, and terribly alone in the world.

What was missing?

No one had ever invited her into a deeper journey with Jesus. Instead, she had been taught how to be a good church member. Here are some of the basics:

- Give mental assent to a few Christian beliefs
- Attend church
- Give some money
- Serve in the church

The Deepest Needs

Although there is nothing wrong with these expectations of church members, they tend to focus on keeping the institution afloat. On their own, they do not touch the deepest needs of a person's heart. In Lauren's case, they did not have the power to address her avoidance of real relationships, her pattern of quitting, her loneliness, or her lack of purpose. An hour on Sunday sitting in rows or watching online simply can't affect that level of change. It was never meant to.

Becoming a "Christian" in this sense failed to help her handle life's challenges. Somehow, the best parts of following Jesus were left out.

- Lauren did not learn how to talk and listen to God or be guided by God's Holy Spirit.
- She missed experiencing God's personal love and forgiveness that comes through faith in Jesus Christ and the joy of sharing that love with others.
- Although her church family loved her, Lauren was not supported by a small group of friends who would accept her as she was and encourage her to grow.
- She did not receive a firm foundation of truth to guide her daily life.

- Though she longed to find herself, no one sat down with Lauren to help her discover her unique calling in God's grander vision.

- Along the way, she was not inspired to give her time and resources to provide healing, justice, and hope to those in need.

Instead of inviting Lauren into these life-shaping practices of a disciple, she was given a facsimile of faith. Mirroring what was modeled for her, she became kinda Christian. Like genuine imitation leather, it looks like the real thing, but under stress, it cracks and breaks. As her life unraveled, Lauren discovered something was missing in her faith journey—something she desperately needed. She bore Christ's name but could not access his power.

Maybe you know someone like Lauren. Many of us have friends or family members who espouse Christian beliefs, even participate in some Christian activities, but their lives are marred by destructive patterns, damaged relationships, and a deep hopelessness that keeps them stuck.

Truth be told, Lauren's story may remind us of our own. It's easy to practice a form of faith without ever experiencing its power. Clear signs are a sense of inner emptiness or persistent discontent—even when life is going well. To our surprise, there's a hole in our soul, and we can't seem to fill it.

Something More

Whether we are agnostic or averse to God, exploring other faiths, or kinda Christian, the common thread that connects us is a search for something beyond ourselves—something that can heal our pain, restore our relationships, and bring joy to our world. Deep down, we long to know if there is a God who sees us and loves us as we are. As curious souls, we wonder, "Is life more than a random smattering of unconnected dots?" The faith of our culture doesn't speak to such things. It offers a dusting of Christianity and billboard platitudes that devolves into "just be nice." We need something more.

C. S. Lewis, beloved author of *The Chronicles of Narnia*, said, "If we find ourselves with a desire that nothing in this world can satisfy, the most probable explanation is that we were made for another world."[1]

---

1. Lewis, C.S, "Reflections: The Desire for My True Country," n.d. C.S. Lewis Institute. Reflections: The Desire For My True Country - C.S. Lewis Institute.

What if that were true? It might explain why Jesus still calls people to follow him. When we become his disciples, we find the only thing that can satisfy our souls—a real relationship with God. But there's more to following Jesus than meets the eye.

In one church I served, we often shared our mission statement in services and small groups: "to make disciples of Jesus Christ for the transformation of the world." To folks on the inside, those twelve words said it all. But over time, more and more newcomers heard that mission and said, "I really like the whole 'transformation of the world' thing, but what's a disciple?"

The question stopped us in our tracks. Until then, we had assumed everyone kind of knew what a disciple was. But to be honest, we didn't have a clear answer either. "Well…some of this. A little of that. Um, we know one when we see one!" That wasn't very helpful.

Finally, I called our pastors together and said, "We need a better answer. We are here to help spiritually curious people discover a deep, personal relationship with Jesus that transforms their lives and the world. That will only happen if we are clear on what a disciple looks like. Besides, how hard could it be? We'll knock this thing out in three weeks."

Eight months later, we finally had something to share with our leaders. It took so much longer than expected because we had to dig deeply into Scripture, into the long-held practices of the church, and into our own guts to ask, "What does it really mean to follow Jesus?"

Deeply Devoted

As we drilled down on that question, some basic characteristics slowly emerged. We longed to see what we called "Deeply Devoted Disciples." These everyday people eagerly engage in instruction and training as an apprentice of Jesus. Along the way, they inwardly experience God's unmerited love while outwardly expressing their personal faith. It's a double ring. Deeply devoted disciples radiate a holy love in heart *and* life. That's life in 3D. It's what Lauren desired but didn't know was possible.

Such disciples can be broadly defined by three core characteristics: loving God unreservedly, launching into community with others, and unleashing compassion to those in need. In short, our call is to:

1. Love God

2. Launch Community

3. Unleash Compassion

As this big picture became clear, the finer points came into focus. We identified six marks of a disciple that ignite our spiritual passion: Glory, Grace, Group, Growth, Giftedness, and Generosity. Since they all started with "G," they became our "G6" network. Over time, we saw how each of the core characteristics connects with two of the G's.

Love God	Launch Community	Unleash Compassion
Glory & Grace	Group & Growth	Giftedness & Generosity

Here's a quick look at the six crucial marks of a deeply devoted disciple:

Glory: *A disciple joyfully and intentionally lives in the presence of God both privately and publicly.*

Grace: *A disciple has personally accepted the unmerited love of God offered in Jesus Christ and intentionally shares Christ's love with those who don't know him yet.*

Group: *A disciple regularly connects with a handful of other disciples to taste grace, apply Scripture, and encourage one another to become like Christ in thought, word, and action.*

Growth: *A disciple takes personal responsibility for his or her spiritual journey by practicing spiritual disciplines that cultivate Christ-centered living and by helping others grow on their journey.*

Giftedness: *A disciple sees his or her identity as a servant of Christ, discovers one's spiritual gifts, deploys them in ministry under God's direction, and develops them to their fullest potential.*

Generosity: *A disciple humbly recognizes all of life belongs to God and cheerfully gives his or her time and resources to bring Christ's healing, justice, and hope to those in need.*

Woven together, these six marks create a beautiful tapestry of deep devotion to Jesus. Over the next six chapters, we will explore how God's Holy Spirit can use them all to fill the hole in our soul. Section Two will focus on creating a regular rhythm of life-giving practices and embracing a practical approach to help others become disciples with us. Every step is part of a transforming journey. I love the way spiritual writer Dallas Willard, describes it:

Discipleship is the process of becoming who Jesus would be if he were you.

As we move through the G's, think of them as essential ingredients of a wedding cake, rather than sequential steps on a staircase. All the ingredients are necessary, but they may be added in various orders based on the needs of each person. It's the sum of the spiritual principles and practices that matter. The G's simply give us a defined path to becoming a disciple of Jesus. To keep our eyes fixed on the goal, here's a one-sentence description to carry with us:

A disciple loves Jesus above all else and loves the world as Jesus does.

While on this journey, it is my hope you will read these pages and engage with the content as part of a small group or class. You may want to go through this material with your family members or a close friend. I've found we always learn more and experience deeper change when we travel together.

Didn't See It Coming

Speaking of change, here's the rest of Lauren's story. Out of the blue, she got invited to a church and reluctantly decided to go. When the pastor talked about discovering a new life through faith in Jesus and doing life together, something happened that Lauren didn't see coming.

> *Somehow, those words broke through the wall I had built up and spoke to the lonely person deep inside me. I suddenly realized I didn't want to remain hidden. I thought maybe this would be a safe place to be known. So, I got involved and stuck around to learn more.*
>
> *Later, I joined an in-depth Bible study group. When we studied the Gospel of John in the New Testament, I found out that Jesus came not only to save my eternal life but also to help me to have an abundant life here on earth. Jesus wanted the very thing that I had never put into words and had only dared to dream about. He wanted me to change the "quitting" pattern in my life and to stick with something—Him! That's when I asked Him into my life, to forgive the mistakes of the past, and to lead me into a better future.*
>
> *Since asking Him into my life, I have had many challenges and opportunities to quit when things got tough. He has taught me the value of seeing things through to their conclusion—a gift I would have never experienced without Him.*

Lauren never knew life could be like this. She has become such an unwavering woman of faith that it has surprised and blessed everyone around her. Choosing to be a disciple of Jesus didn't just change her heart. It has changed her life.

Taking Jesus' love seriously will likely change us too. Let's start by learning how to joyfully enter God's presence.

SECTION ONE

Deeply Devoted Disciples

God Up Close

So, whether you eat or drink or whatever you do,
do everything for the glory of God.

—1 Corinthians 10:31 NRSVUE

We have no design but to promote the glory of God.

—John Wesley

I didn't know this could happen.

When I was 24, I served as an associate pastor-intern at a church in Austin, Texas. Graciously, the congregation provided a house for me directly across the street from the church. The living room doubled as an adult Sunday school class, but the rest of the time, this small, two-bedroom home sat empty. It was the perfect place for a single guy who wouldn't mind people barging in unannounced at any time, day or night, to grab something out of the kitchen or ask me to unlock the church after hours. (It's the rent you pay.)

One night, I went to sleep in my back bedroom around 11:00, as usual. I'm typically a very sound sleeper, but that night, I suddenly woke up around 2:30 in the morning. There was no loud noise. My alarm hadn't gone off. No one was at the door. But for some reason, I was wide awake. And I wasn't alone. Someone had entered the room.

With my heart in my throat, I slowly turned on the light by my bed. I half expected to see somebody standing three feet away, but no one was there, physically.

For some unknown reason, the Holy Spirit paid me a visit that night. I sat up in my bed and soaked in one of the most beautiful moments of my life. Warmth and peace enveloped the room.

1

At one point, I experienced a love so deep and personal, it brought tears to my eyes. I wanted to talk to God, but what came out of my heart instead was singing. I was so thankful I didn't know what to say.

Eventually, I asked God, "Why are you here? I don't deserve this. I am *so* unworthy." But I received no response. No one had taught me how to listen back then. All I knew about prayer was the talking part.

Finally, after about 30 minutes, I said, "Thank you, Lord. Thank you for being with me. Stay as long as you want, but I'm starting to fall asleep." And I slowly nodded off.

The next morning, the Presence was gone. To this day, I don't know why God showed up so unexpectedly in my bedroom that night. I hadn't prayed for it. I didn't know you could ask for something like that. It wasn't a dream. I was as awake as I am while writing these words. It was 100 percent real.

Although that was many years ago, I've never had an experience quite like it since. For decades, I chose not to tell this story. I figured people would think I had lost it, but you may have guessed that by now. I only share it here because it was one of my most vivid experiences of God's glory.

The word "glory" comes from the Latin word *Gloria*, which means fame or renown. It is a transforming display of God's presence. "Glory" is found over 250 times in the Bible.

Scripture says, "the earth will be filled with the knowledge of the glory of the LORD, as the waters cover the sea" (Habakkuk 2:14 NRSVUE).

John tells us that Jesus, God's Son, "lived among us, and we have seen his glory" (John 1:14 NRSVUE).

Paul told the early Christians, the mystery of the gospel is "Christ in you, the hope of glory" (Colossians 1:27).

In other words, the glory of God is designed to dwell richly in God's creation. Consider that for a moment. By the Spirit of Jesus residing in our lives, the Creator and Ruler of the Universe shines his glory through people like us. Wild!

In the Old Testament, the Hebrew word for glory is *Kabod*. It's original meaning is "weight" or "heaviness"—the *Kabod* of God. I love the ring of it. *Kabod* also expresses importance, honor, and majesty.

This sense of grandeur shows up powerfully in a conversation Moses had with God. In the second book of the Bible, Moses had just received the 10 commandments on Mt. Sinai. At God's direction, he now faced the enormous task of leading two million Israelites from Mt. Sinai through the desert to the promised land.

The burden weighed so heavily that Moses pleaded with the Lord, "...show me your ways, so that I may know you and find favor in your sight. Consider, too, that this nation is your people."[1]

God simply responds, "My presence will go with you."[2]

Still anxious and needing more, Moses makes a gutsy ask,

"Please show me your glory."

—*Exodus 33:18 NRSVUE*

Keep in mind, not long before on that very mountain, Moses stood barefoot before a burning bush. He knew firsthand the empowering peace of the Presence when called to a daunting task. But his request to *see* God's glory was riskier than he realized.

The Lord replied, "I will cause all my goodness to pass in front of you... But... you cannot see my face, for no one may see me and live."[3]

Out of compassion, God made this provision,

When my glory passes by, I will put you in a cleft in the rock and cover you with my hand until I have passed by. Then I will remove my hand and you will see my back; but my face must not be seen.

—*Exodus 33:22–23*

So powerful was God's glory, Moses had to be protected from seeing too much of it. It's no accident that in nearly every divine/human encounter in the Bible, God begins by saying, "Do not be afraid."

It's our natural response. When the angel Gabriel came to a teenage peasant girl named Mary, she was "greatly troubled."[4] Seeing her alarm, Gabriel said, "Do not be afraid, Mary; you have found favor with God."[5]

A few months later, while tending their sheep one night, some shepherds encountered the fearsome power of God's glory. Their reaction was typical.

An angel of the Lord appeared to them, and the glory of the Lord shone around them, and they were terrified.

—*Luke 2:9*

---

1. Exodus 33:13 NRSVUE
2. Exodus 33:14 NRSVUE
3. Exodus 33:19–20
4. Luke 1:29
5. Luke 1:30

3

Why so much fear? God's glory is so holy, so pure, so full of truth that it shines a floodlight on every dark place in us that falls short. That unrelenting light is so overwhelming, it triggers our most primal fear: death. Instinctively, we say to ourselves, "If I'm exposed to this piercing purity too long, I will cease to exist."

But God's glory is not revealed to wipe us off the earth; it's to wrap us in his love. When we allow the truth, beauty, and love of the Presence to touch our hearts, it does not erase our existence. It enlivens every part of it.

The supreme display of God's glory came in Jesus. Near the end of his life, Jesus prays to his Heavenly Father:

> *I glorified you on earth by finishing the work that you gave me to do. So now, Father, glorify me* in your own presence *with the* glory *that I had in your presence before the world existed.*
>
> —*John 17:4–5 NRSVUE (Emphasis added)*

Jesus understood this intimately: the Presence carries the glory. All through Scripture, we see the same pattern played out in people like Moses, Mary, and the shepherds. *When we encounter God's presence, we experience God's glory.*

Perhaps you have noticed a deep hunger in yourself and others for a personal experience of God. Many of us have moved beyond a desire to know something intellectually. We want to experience things on a soul level. When it comes to God, we want a divine encounter. *"Please show me your glory."*[6] We want God up close.

Jesus says that's what God wants too. God is looking for worshippers. People who will worship God in spirit and in truth.[7]

But we can't make God meet us on our commute or in the school cafeteria or in the coziness of our bedroom. All we can do is engage in certain practices and invite God to show up. Let's explore some time-tested ways to enter the Presence and stay connected.

Staying Connected

Many people have felt God up close in a large worship experience. A while back, the church I was serving hosted a community-wide Sunday night service with Bob Goff, the New York Times bestselling author of *Love Does* and other popular books.

---

6. Exodus 33:18 NRSVUE

7. John 4:23

Over a thousand people packed the place that night. The energy in the room was electric! Worship leaders from five churches across the city led us to the throne room of God. With our hearts opened wide, we heard a man from our church share an astonishing God encounter that completely changed the trajectory of his life. Bob Goff then hit a grand slam with his talk about loving people.

At one point, Bob threw off his shoes and humbly gave the rest of his talk in his socks. His simple message from Scripture resonated deeply: *live in grace, walk in love.* People practically floated out of the sanctuary that night. We knew God's glory had passed by.

Of course, not every worship experience lights up the room. After one service, a woman came up to her pastor and said, "I hope you didn't take it personally, Pastor, when my husband walked out during your sermon."

The pastor replied, "I did find it a little disconcerting."

She said, "It's not a reflection on you, Pastor. Richard has been walking in his sleep ever since he was a child."

What's your experience of God in the big room? I asked some friends to share what it's like for them.

One woman said, "Sunday worship for me is utter release. I am so caught up in the 'world' all week, and I usually can't wait for church. There are times I am so moved by the Holy Spirit while singing that I can't even sing anymore. I am so overwhelmed with the words and feelings of gratitude all I can do is cry. I have NEVER felt like this before."

A man said, "Services at our church refresh my spirit and energize me for the week ahead. They also challenge me to be intentional about my Christian beliefs."

Someone who had come to worship for just a few months said, "A friend asked me to try her church one Sunday. When I walked into the sanctuary a feeling came over me like I've never had before. I was home. It was around the holidays, so the front was covered in pine trees and was very festive and inviting. When the music started, I had goose bumps, and I had them the entire service. I've never felt that way in church. I started attending every Sunday, and now I even go to a small group before the service."

For many people, the biggest problem with worship is it only happens once a week. But it wasn't designed to be that way.

Over the centuries, the church has turned worshipping God into a ritual done in a certain place at a certain time led by a certain group of people.

5

While there are great benefits to a weekly practice of corporate worship, a single hour or so of institutionally organized and professionally led "worship" was never the original design.

What God really wants from us is not ritual but relationship. God wants a deep, two-way love relationship with you and me. I love the way 14th century Eastern Orthodox writer Kallistos Katafygiotis describes this:

> *The most important thing that happens between God and the human soul is to love and to be loved.*[8]

Consciously living in the presence of that love is true worship. It goes beyond our intellect and engages us on a heart level. The Apostle Paul, a man of great learning, wrote to the early Christians in Ephesus:

> *And I pray that you, being rooted and established in love, may have power…to grasp how wide and long and high and deep is the love of Christ, and to* know *this love that surpasses knowledge—that you may be filled to the measure of all the fullness of God.*

> *—Ephesians 3:17–19 (Emphasis added)*

Paul is praying for them to experience God's glorious presence through Christ's expansive love. It's not about espousing *precepts*. It's about encountering a *person*—Jesus.

For followers of Jesus, worship is not an event; it's a *lifestyle*. Worship was never intended to be something you could drive to, sit through, and go home from, nor was it designed to be passively watched while logged on. Living in an ongoing, loving relationship with God is a way of life. It's the way of a disciple.

> *A deeply devoted disciple intentionally lives in the presence of God, not just publicly but privately.*

At their best, public services are intended to ignite our private worship of God in the other 167 hours of our week. We don't ever have to leave the presence of God.

Many people throughout history have discovered this secret. In the 17th century, there was a little-known man who served kitchen duty in a mon-

---

8. Kallistos, Bishop of Diokleia, *The Orthodox Way*, Crestwood, Ny: St. Vladimir's Seminary Press, 1995.

astery in Paris for many years. He was ordinary in all ways except one: how closely he walked with God in every circumstance of life. In his words,

> *The time of busyness does not with me differ from the time of prayer; and in the noise and clatter of my kitchen, while several persons are at the same time calling for different things, I possess God in as great tranquility as if I were upon my knees before the Blessed Sacrament.*[9]

Known as Brother Lawrence, this man's life and faith were so inspiring that everyone around him wanted to know God the way he did. After he died, his friends put together a little book of his letters and conversations called *The Practice of the Presence of God*. Outside of the Bible, it is thought to be the most widely read book in the last three centuries.

To help his friends visualize this practice, Brother Lawrence talked about the chapel of our hearts.

> *It isn't necessary that we stay in church in order to remain in God's presence. We can make our hearts personal chapels where we can enter anytime to talk to God privately. These conversations can be so loving and gentle, and anyone can have them.*[10]

Turning our hearts into chapels of worship perfectly fits Jesus' vision for his followers. He desires his disciples to stay connected to his presence. It is how we experience his glory and live out his purpose for us. He invites us to mutually share our life with him.

> *Abide in me as I abide in you. Just as the branch cannot bear fruit by itself unless it abides in the vine, neither can you unless you abide in me. I am the vine; you are the branches. Those who abide in me and I in them bear much fruit, because apart from me you can do nothing.*
>
> *— John 15:4–5 NRSVUE*

To abide is to be present. It also means to dwell, to remain, and to be held and kept. When we abide in him, we trust moment by moment that we are loved. Nothing in the shifting sands of circumstances or people's varying opinions about us matter in Jesus' eyes. Not even our own sin or self doubts can change his love for us. True abiding brings deep peace.

---

9. Attributed to Brother Lawrence, *The Practice of the Presence of God*.

10. Brother Lawrence, *The Practice of the Presence of God*, Whitaker House, 1982, p. 37.

Imagine what it would be like to live out of a deeply poised center. What could that kind of peace do for a marriage, a parent-child bond, or a relationship with a boss, a co-worker, or someone with whom we strongly disagree? It's a revolutionary way of being.

How could we turn our hearts into personal chapels? Here are three proven practices:

- **Experience God in daily solitude**

For years, I missed it.

Sandwiched between scenes where Jesus cleanses a leper, massive crowds press in to hear him teach, and friends of a paralytic man lower him through a roof to be healed, there is a short verse. With all the other action in the story, many people skip right over it. I know I did, until one day it caught my attention.

> *But Jesus often withdrew to lonely places and prayed.*
>
> *—Luke 5:16*

In the busiest season of his life, when everyone was clamoring for his attention, this single sentence speaks volumes about how to live as Jesus lived. He intentionally stopped to be alone with God.

Jesus didn't do this occasionally. The word that caught my eye was *often*. If the Son of God needed to steal away for alone time with God *often*, what does that mean for us?

Asked in a different way, do you know anyone who is still lugging around the same problems they had at this time last year? Twelve months have gone by, but the situation they face at home, the problems they have at work, the personal issues they struggle with inside haven't changed a bit. It's as if time stood still.

A lack of progress is the curse of hurry. Living life in a blur allows no time to think, no time to check our emotional, spiritual, and relational gauges, and no time to make needed course corrections. There is only time to do. Too often, speed does not get us down the road faster; it takes us down the wrong road. As author David Fleming put it,

> *Forward movement is not helpful if what is needed is a change of direction.*[11]

---

11. Fleming, David, *Lean logic: A Dictionary for the Future and How to Survive It*, White River Junction, VT: Chelsea Green Publishing, 2016.

Oddly enough, ceaseless motion is both dangerous and monotonous. Not only does it cut us off from the presence of God—a perilous place both spiritually and morally—it also reduces the potential for real change to zero. We get stuck making the same mistakes, committing the same sins, and clinging to the same routines, no matter how harmful or unproductive they may be.

In Scripture, the Creator of the universe says,

> *Be still, and know that I am God.*
>
> *—Psalm 46:10*

Mercifully, God commands us to put away our anxious doing and endless attempts to control, so we can know God's personal love and infinite power. Non-stop activity is not the dwelling place of our God. God is known in stillness.

That's why it's so critical to carve out a regular time and a regular place to be alone with God. It's a daily rhythm that allows us to recalibrate our souls.

Solitude is a simple practice. I outlined it in a previous book this way:

1. Set aside some time alone each day. It's easiest if you set the same time every day. That way you can build it into your schedule as a habit.

2. Find a quiet place apart from interruptions. Anything with an "on" button needs to be turned off. If possible, go to the same place each day.

3. Find a comfortable position. Feel free to stand, sit, or kneel. You may prefer a solitary walk in nature.

4. As you begin, notice your breathing. Put yourself in tune with the rhythms of your body. Take some deep breaths. Relax.

5. Release any worries or concerns. You may put your palms down and symbolically let them go.

6. Receive. Listen quietly for the messages your body, your emotions, your spirit, and God have to say. You may put your palms up as a sign of receiving.[12]

---

12. Ross, Roger, *Come Back: Returning to the Life You Were Made For*, Nashville, TN: Abingdon Press, 2020, p. 35.

If this form of prayer is a new practice, start small. Occasional joggers do not run marathons. Begin with five or ten minutes a day. As it becomes a habit, these solitude sessions can be increased. Spending regular time in the chapel of our hearts will not only reveal messages from God about our lives, it will also help us live each day out of a deeply poised center.

Of course, slowing down is subversive in our culture. We tend to look up to the person who is in demand and always on the go. But no one can change a flat tire while going 90 miles an hour. To change the tire, we have to stop the car. I've found that continual motion is a dead end. Ironically, the busiest people in life are the deadest. Those who never stop never grow.

A second way to practice the Presence involves an inner conversation.

- **Experience God in ongoing dialogue**

In a letter to the early Christians, the Apostle Paul says,

Pray without ceasing.

—1 Thessalonians 5:17 NRSVUE

Ever wondered, "How on earth can a person pray continuously? Do you stay on your knees all day? Do you neglect your kids, quit your job, and stop running errands? How do you pray and eat a hamburger at the same time? And if you are too busy praying to pay the bills, check email, do laundry, or talk to a client, do you make other people do that stuff for you? Nobody can pray all the time without becoming a monk on a hill. It is totally impractical."

I confess: for a long time it didn't make sense—but Brother Lawrence helped me see it differently. He told his friends the worst trial he could imagine was losing his sense of God's presence.[13] In his experience, to be constantly aware of God's presence, one must form the habit of continually talking with him throughout each day. We don't need to abandon conversation with God to deal with our day-to-day affairs. Those are precisely the times we need God's guidance the most.[14]

Too true. Perhaps like me, you know the unnecessary pain of dealing with sticky issues apart from an ongoing conversation with God. I don't want that experience anymore. There is a deeper and firmer place to stand. In his

---

13. Brother Lawrence, *The Practice of the Presence of God*, Whitaker House, 1982, p. 21.

14. Ibid., p. 12.

classic little book, *A Testament of Devotion*, Thomas Kelly reveals that place as he explains "The Light Within:"

There is a way of ordering our mental life on more than one level at once. On one level we may be thinking, discussing, seeing, calculating, meeting all the demands of external affairs. But deep within, behind the scenes, at a profounder level, we may also be in prayer and adoration, song and worship and a gentle receptiveness to divine breathings.[15]

Frankly, anyone who has ever fallen in love has had this experience to some degree. Regardless of the outward demands of the moment, there's a sweet song underneath singing, "I am loved. I am valued. I am wanted by my beloved!"

Kelly goes on to describe the relationship between surface living and what he calls the inner sanctuary of the soul:

Between the two levels is fruitful interplay, but ever the accent must be upon the deeper level, where the soul ever dwells in the presence of the Holy One. For the religious [person] is forever bringing all affairs of the first level down into the Light, holding them there in the Presence, reseeing them and the whole of the world of [people] and things in a new and overturning way, and responding to them in spontaneous, incisive and simple ways of love and faith.[16]

Understanding these two levels and their relationship with each other opens a whole new vista in spirituality. Apparently, a person *can* pray without ceasing! Kelly more deeply explains what Brother Lawrence described centuries before. We don't have to quit doing everything else so we can pray, nor do we have to stop praying to get some work done. Life and prayer can happen simultaneously.

We are designed for a 24/7 relationship with God. Like a song that keeps playing in our heads while we do a hundred other things, it is possible to sing in our souls even amid frantic activity.

In addition to continual conversation, another way to cultivate a ceaseless relationship with God is through repeating a word or brief phrase as we breathe. These "breath prayers" can be as simple as "Jesus" or "Abba" (the Aramaic word for "Daddy used by Jesus when he prayed to his Father). Possible

---

15. Kelly, Thomas R., *A Testament of Devotion*, San Francisco: HarperCollins, 1992.

16. Ibid.

phrases are "The Lord is my Shepherd," "I receive Your grace," "Lord, have mercy on me," or countless others the Spirit may reveal to you.

As we repeatedly say a word or a phrase in rhythm with our breathing, they start to "pray themselves" without our conscious effort. Through this two-level living, we can ceaselessly pray and adore God regardless of how hectic our day may be.

To be honest, I am still on the front edge of an unceasing prayer life. I've experimented enough to know it is possible to worship in the chapel of my heart through stretches of my day. My goal is to offer God seamless praise. No doubt, this will be a longer journey.

A third way to practice the Presence is through reflection.

- **Experience God in daily review**

This practice addresses an issue many of us have asked about for years. How do we recognize the way God is moving in our lives? Every day is filled with people and activities of all kinds. Where is God in the routine of life?

This very question led Ignatius of Loyola to create the spiritual practice of examen 500 years ago. As the founder of the Jesuits, Ignatius wanted a daily practice to help the society's missionaries notice God's presence in the ordinary moments of their days.

The word *examen* is Latin for "self-knowledge" or "examination." It is a prayer of reflection that invites us to watch the game tape of our day with God. Either in the evening or at the beginning of the next day, this 5R prayer exercise will help us see where God has been moving.

1. Relish—Offer thanksgiving to God for all the joys, as well as the challenges, of the day that come to mind.

2. Request—Ask God for light to help you see all that happened in your day through God's eyes.

3. Review—Play the movie of the day just lived. Start from the moment your eyes opened. Notice the times and interactions when you sensed a surge of life. When did you feel love, joy, and hope? These are movements toward God. Identify what was happening in and around you during those experiences. Conversely, notice the times in the day when you sensed discouragement, disconnection, or emptiness. At these moments,

you were moving away from God. Your spirit was getting colder, not warmer. What was behind that?

4. Response—In light of the review, ask, "How am I led to respond to the God of my life? Where do I need to ask for forgiveness? Is God leading me to someone in need?"

5. Renewal—As you look forward to the day ahead, what feelings about the next 24 hours do you need to bring before God? What spirit do you want to carry into the new day?

With just a few minutes of reflection each day, we can uncover significant moments of consolation and desolation in our lives. Experiences of consolation are from God. They draw us into closer union with the lover of our soul. Times of desolation are from the enemy of our soul. They create distance in our relationship with God.

The genius of the examen rests in Ignatius' insight that our ordinary human experiences provide invaluable information about God's activity in our lives. Yet apart from intentional reflection, that activity often goes unnoticed. As we engage in this prayer practice over time, we will become more adept at recognizing how God is moving throughout our day.

Someone might say, "That sounds great, but what's the practical benefit of recognizing the movement of God?" Perhaps the best answer is another question: *Have you ever had a big decision to make?*

If any of us have ever struggled over what career path to take, what technical school or college to attend, whether we should take a certain job, if we should move, whether to get married, who to marry, whether to stay married, if we should have children, how to raise a child, when to seek professional help, whether to do a business deal, how to handle our money, whether to take legal action, when to stop medical care for a loved one, when to retire, where to retire, when to move into a nursing facility, or hundreds of other major decisions, we have some sense of why this issue matters. Learning to discern where God is moving (and where God is not) can save us from some disastrous life turns. The lover of our soul always wants the best for us and is more than willing to reveal next steps, if we will take the time to *examen* our lives and listen.

Taken together, these three practices—daily solitude, ongoing conversation, and daily review—can revolutionize our spiritual lives. As we use these

13

tools to build the chapel of our hearts, we are making a 24/7 dwelling place for the Spirit of Jesus, the Holy Spirit, to abide in us as we abide in him.

It's there that we experience "Christ in us, the hope of glory" (Colossians 1:27). Our hope not only includes the promise of future glory with God in heaven. It's also a present reality that shapes our lives now.

Here's the bonus: as we experience God's glory, we discover God's grace, and frankly, it's amazing.

Grace Awakening

Make sure that no one misses out on God's grace.

—Hebrews 12:15 CEB

You have never lived one unloved moment in your life.

—Anita Renfroe

It was an unguarded moment.

A woman in her mid-30s had applied for a position in a church-related organization. Amanda happily answered questions about her background and work history. Our interview team was impressed with her poise and professionalism. At one point, someone asked, "Can you tell us a little about your spiritual journey?"

She took a deep breath, smiled nervously, and said, "I thought you might ask about that."

She looked down and softly replied, "I don't really have one. My family never went to church much when I was growing up, and the kids and I rarely go now. I don't know why..."

Her words had a confessional tone. The issue had restlessly dangled in her heart for years.

"A couple of months ago," she continued, "I was talking to one of my friends about my life, and out of the blue, she said, '*You seem like a lost soul.*' The more I thought about it, the more I realized she was right. I do feel lost— like I'm missing something."

Unexpectedly, tears filled Amanda's eyes. As she grabbed a tissue, she said, "I want to believe. I just haven't found a... connection."

For a moment, the room fell silent. Interviews aren't usually that revealing. After everyone took a breath, we thanked her for sharing so vulnerably. We also assured her she was not alone.

Untold millions share Amanda's deep longing to connect with God. Author Philip Yancey tells of a therapist who keeps a running list of the complaints his clients share each day: "emptiness, vague depression, a yearning for personal fulfillment, a hunger for spirituality – all of which he diagnoses as a 'loss of soul,' a void that modern culture fails to satisfy with its lure of entertainment and material goods."[1]

In our relentless pursuit of more, we're left with less of what we desire most—joy, purpose, and connection. The only known antidote for such inner loss is grace—the unmerited love of God poured into an empty soul.

Yet we face a staggering dilemma. Our world is so divided over so many things it feels like grace is in short supply. How can we recover the core of the Christian faith and offer it to people who feel a hole in their soul? What if, through our own journey with Jesus, we become grace-filled people who easily pour God's unmerited love into anyone who yearns for it—perhaps someone like Amanda? That's how God designed grace to work. *A disciple has personally accepted the unmerited love of God offered in Jesus Christ and intentionally shares Christ's love with those who don't know Him yet.*

When we experience this kind of divine love, we are far more likely to offer it to those around us. Imagine what a gift that could be to our world!

Let's begin by experiencing the offer ourselves.

Grace Matters

Jesus was a master at pouring out grace. The first four books of the Bible's New Testament describe Jesus' life and teaching. They are filled with stories of grace—stories that often led to jaws dropping. This scene from Luke is no exception.

One day, a strict religious leader invited Jesus to a dinner party. In those days, people reclined on couches around a low table. Like everyone else,

---

1. Yancey, Philip, *Vanishing Grace: What Ever Happened to the Good News?*, Grand Rapids, MI: Zondervan, 2014, p. 32.

Jesus' feet were behind him, away from the table. Everything was going as planned—until an unexpected guest crashed the party.

A woman in that town who lived a sinful life learned that Jesus was eating at the Pharisee's house, so she came there with an alabaster jar of perfume. As she stood behind him at his feet weeping, she began to wet his feet with her tears. Then she wiped them with her hair, kissed them and poured perfume on them.

—Luke 7:37–38

Talk about uncomfortable. All conversation stopped. The Pharisee who had invited Jesus said to himself,

"If this man were a prophet, he would know who is touching him and what kind of woman she is—that she is a sinner."

—Luke 7:39

Sensing his thoughts, Jesus addressed his new friend directly.

"Simon, I have something to tell you... Two people owed money to a certain moneylender. One owed him five hundred denarii, and the other fifty. Neither of them had the money to pay him back, so he forgave the debts of both. Now which of them will love him more?"

—Luke 7:40–42

Simon responded, "The one who was forgiven more, I suppose."

Jesus said, "You are correct. "Now, Simon, look at this woman. When I came into your house, you didn't give me any water for my feet (a minimal gesture of hospitality in a hot and arid climate), yet she washed my feet with her tears, wiping them with her hair.

"You didn't give me a kiss (a common sign of welcome and friendship in the Middle East), but she hasn't stopped kissing my feet.

"Nor did you put oil on my head (another sign of welcome and acceptance), but she poured perfume on my feet"[2]

Therefore, I tell you, her many sins have been forgiven—as her great love has shown. But whoever has been forgiven little loves little.

—Luke 7:47

---

2. Author's paraphrase and commentary on Luke 7:43-46.

I can only imagine Simon was left speechless but not for the reason we might think. For most of my life, I missed Jesus' deeper point. We intuitively get the initial one. The greater the forgiveness, the greater one's love for the forgiver.

The power of grace in this woman's life is unmistakable. She was likely a prostitute in that town. Well known for her profession, the upright religious people considered her an outcast. It may have been years since she darkened the door of a Synagogue. There was no room for sinners like her.

But at some point, she must have heard Jesus preach along a roadside or on a hill, as he often did. Somehow, something he said touched her deep inside.

Contrary to what she had been told, she was not hopeless or forgotten or a soulless piece of meat that could be bought and sold. She was a precious daughter of God. She was loved, she could be forgiven, and her life could be redeemed. The thought brought tears to her eyes. For far too long, she had judged her worth by how much a man would pay for her.

In contrast to every other voice in her life, she heard from Jesus, "You are loved. You have infinite worth in the eyes of God." Naturally, as someone forgiven beyond her wildest dreams, she felt great love for her forgiver.

On the flipside is Simon. He's very religious. He prides himself on knowing and following all the rules. He prays the prayers, attends worship every week, and chairs the Administrative Board. His standing in the Synagogue is well known. To be honest, he's so moral, his sins-to-be-forgiven list is pretty short. Small wonder he loves little.

Here's where I missed Jesus' crucial point. It's not that the woman had many sins, and Simon had few. Nor is it that she had BIG sins, and he had little ones.

It's that she recognized her need for forgiveness, while Simon, in his self-righteousness, thought he didn't need it. He assumed he could save himself by his goodness. And that was his biggest sin.

As author Timothy Keller explains it, "In Jesus' Gospel, everyone is wrong. Everyone is loved, and everyone is called to recognize this and change."[3]

---

3. Keller, Timothy, *The Prodigal God: Recovering the Heart of the Christian Faith*, NY, NY: Penguin Books, 2016, p. 45.

Turns out, the only way to receive the grace of God is to know we need it.[4] The woman in this story got that. That's why Jesus said to her,

"Your faith has saved you; go in peace."

—*Luke 7:50*

If you grew up in church like I did, this is the hardest thing to understand about God's grace. Like Simon, many of us believe, "If I obey, then I will earn God's love." It's our default mode.[5] Upright religious people often wonder, "Doesn't God owe me something for my goodness?"

The whole concept of being loved apart from our merits seems senseless, but to be loved even when we act badly—it just doesn't seem fair. And, of course, it's not. It is better. Scripture says we have all sinned and the consequence of our sin is death, both physical and spiritual, forever.[6] Once we come to terms with our true state before God, clamoring for what we deserve is a terrible strategy. Thankfully, God gives us what we don't deserve: grace.

I like the way spiritual writer Max Lucado says it:

If I'm better tomorrow, I won't be loved more.
If I'm worse tomorrow, I won't be loved less.
God's love does not ebb and flow or come and go.

This is the stunning good news of Jesus. Unlike us, he does not divide the world into immoral "bad guys" and moral "good guys"[7]—people who really need to be forgiven and people who don't need it much. The latter category does not exist. We are all powerless to save ourselves.

When tempted to think otherwise, take a quick inventory. Have you ever decided to go on a diet, then gained three pounds after the first week? Perhaps you know you shouldn't watch a certain movie or streaming service, but you can't seem to stay away from it. Maybe you have caught yourself saying, "That's it, I am never going to say anything bad about that person again. I can't help that he's an idiot."

---

4.   Ibid.

5.   Ibid., p. 114.

6.   Romans 3:23, 6:23

7.   Keller, Timothy, *The Prodigal God: Recovering the Heart of the Christian Faith*, NY, NY: Penguin Books, 2016, p. 44.

Perhaps you've said, "I know our finances are tight, and I agreed not to buy anything right now, but when I saw that deluxe, imported coffee maker, it was *calling* to me."

Deep down, you don't want to go to that internet site again or keep making excuses to talk to that really attractive person at work. You know where such things will lead. But you can't stop yourself.

You're not alone. Paul, who wrote over half of the New Testament, said,

I do not understand my own actions. For I do not do what I want, but I do the very thing I hate.

—Romans 7:15 NRSVUE

What's going on here? Below our awareness, there's a power at work within us that is stronger than our willpower. It's a dark force that seeks to undermine our lives. It leads us to places we don't want to go and to do things we don't want to do—in some cases, the very things we hate. The Bible calls it a sinful nature, and it renders us powerless to save ourselves.

In his letter to the early Christians in Ephesus, Paul described how this power works in our lives.

Once you were dead because of your disobedience and your many sins. You used to live in sin, just like the rest of the world, obeying...the spirit at work in the hearts of those who refuse to obey God. All of us used to live that way, following the passionate desires and inclinations of our sinful nature.

—Ephesians 2:1–3 NLT

When Paul says, "Before you knew Christ, you were dead," he's not talking about a zombie apocalypse. Pre-conversion, these people were holding down jobs, raising families, going to school, and more, but spiritually, they were like a boat that had lost its engine. They were dead in the water, drifting with the currents of the culture and buffeted by the waves of unruly desires.

Many of us can relate. We may have found ourselves frantically busy on the outside while feeling dead on the inside. Caught in behaviors that are pulling us down, we just don't have the power to right our own ship. Life with no engine leads to constant battering against the rocks. Over time, this experience is so painful, we begin to wonder if God is against us.

Finally, we conclude our life is not working, so we take matters into our own hands. "Clearly, I am not trying hard enough," a little voice says in our head. So we set out to fix that. But it doesn't work the way we think it will.

David Prince tells of a family who adopted an older child from a horrendous orphanage in another country. When they brought their new daughter home, they told her as part of this new family, she was expected to clean her room every day. She immediately fixated on that responsibility and saw it as a ticket to earning her family's love. Each morning, when her parents came into her room, it was pristine. She would sit on the bed, look up, and say, "My room is clean. Can I stay? Do you still love me?"

Her attempts to be loved broke her new parents' hearts.[8] They break God's heart, too—though we get the logic.

"I know I can't change what I've said and done in the past," we may say, "but if I do enough good things, maybe God will love me."

It's called the Works Plan. The premise is simple: "If I do enough good works, I can offset my sins and earn God's favor." Deep down, many of us keep a running tab of good works versus bad to ensure the scale tips toward God's approval. *Can I stay? Do you still love me?*

However, the plan itself is flawed. In the spiritual realm, good works don't offset sins. Think about a marriage relationship. If a husband is unfaithful, it doesn't matter how many times he empties the dishwasher or takes out the garbage. His good works can't erase his unfaithfulness. We can't work off sins. The only way to remove a sin is through forgiveness. And for that, we need outside help.

The Works Plan hits close to home for me. Growing up, I was a boy scout Christian. I kept my nose clean, came to church, helped a few little old ladies across the street, and thought I was in.

Like Simon, I was trying to earn the salvation God was giving away for free. Here's what I didn't understand: it's not about what we can do for God but what God can do for us. Let's pick up Paul's letter again.

> *But God is so rich in mercy, and he loved us so much, that even though we were dead because of our sins, he gave us life when he raised Christ from the dead. (It is only by God's grace that you have been saved!)*
>
> *—Ephesians 2:4–5 NLT*

---

8. Prince, David E., "How Biblical Application Really Works," *Preaching Today*, Skills Article, January 2018, www.preachingtoday.com, Accessed 6-16-25.

For Paul, grace is God's unmerited love offered in Jesus Christ. It carries two profound spiritual benefits. First, through Jesus' victory over sin and death, God forgives us of our sins on a personal level.

- **God's forgiveness of my sins**

When the weight of sin is lifted, we often feel loved for who we are. This is usually the moment we say "Yes" to God and start following Jesus as our Savior. But there is a second part to grace.

- **God's power to change my life**

Grace is also a spiritual power that enables us to live a different kind of life, a holy life, the kind of life we can't make happen by mere human effort.

For those of us who have tried hard to follow all the rules, this is good news! Rule-following may keep us out of trouble in the short term, but it never delivers what it promises. Our goodness does not force God to love us or do our bidding; God already loves us and wants the best for us. Nor does rule-following lead to a life of love, joy, and peace.

Instead, manufacturing our own righteousness produces a "better-than" attitude. Apart from grace, rule-followers inevitably become hard-hearted, irritable, and judgmental. It's the power of God's unmerited love that saves us from that fate. Paul puts it this way:

For it is by God's grace that you have been saved through faith. It is not the result of your own efforts, but God's gift, so that no one can boast about it.

—Ephesians 2:8–9 GNT

Receive The Love

God's love comes to us not by our own efforts but by receiving the gift of grace through faith. Here's how we can do that.

- **First, *admit* that nothing I do or have done can earn my salvation.**

Oddly enough, the Works Plan doesn't work. Trying to earn God's favor by doing good things doesn't deal with our core need for forgiveness or give us the power to live a Christ-like life. Good works are not the root of our salvation; they are the fruit of it. They naturally flow out of a real relationship with God.

In fact, there is nothing you or I can do to make God love us more than God does right now. Pause for a moment and let that sink in. *There is nothing you or I can do to make God love us more than God does right now.* In the same way, there is nothing we can do to make God love us less.

God's love is a gift. It is offered apart from what we have done, who we have done it with, or where we have been. We cannot be bad enough to lose God's love or good enough to earn it. Grace is the one true constant in the universe. For those who are ready, the first step to receiving this grace is to admit we need it.

- **Second, *accept* God's acceptance of me.**

"You've been pre-approved!" The words were blazoned across a promo letter in my mailbox. They made it so easy.[9] I didn't have to prove my financial worth or verify that I was a good risk. That work had already been done. All I needed to do was accept the already made offer.

In the same way, through Christ's work on the cross, we have all been pre-approved. The price for our sins has already been paid. We don't have to clean up our act or draw up a spiritual resume. God has already accepted us. We literally have nothing left to prove. All we need to do is accept God's acceptance of us.

That's grace. Once received, it changes a person from the inside out. As that happens, we naturally want to take the next step.

- **Third, *acknowledge* Christ as the leader of my life.**

This is the toughest part for independent, self-made people. The last thing we want to do is turn control of our lives over to anyone. Frankly, it's scary. Does Jesus really know what's better for me that I do?

We're certainly good with being accepted and forgiven. Deep down, we know we need it, but who wants to give up calling the shots? We'd rather have Jesus as our co-pilot—someone who backs us up, helps us be a success, and makes life more comfortable.

But Jesus has a different seat in mind—the one we are holding onto so tightly. To give up that spot, we will need to resolve these questions: "Is he

---

9. Unfortunately, these credit card offers have been a financial snare for some people.

trustworthy? Is Jesus really God's Son, who sacrificed his life for my sake so I could have life to the fullest?[10] If so, can I trust him with my life?"

Spiritual writer John Ortberg puts it this way, "The only way into the spiritual life is to surrender – to die to our ego, our self-will and our demand to have our own way and have the world revolve around us."[11]

In other words, we must part with the pilot's seat. When we give Jesus the wheel, he will take us to people and places we can't imagine right now. That's his specialty. Following Jesus is a never-ending adventure because he is always leading us to a place we've never been before. Each time we step out in faith, we learn to trust him a little more. And that's when grace flows into our lives.

Relay The Love

To Jesus, God's grace was a feast not meant for a few seats but for the whole world's table. After his resurrection, he revealed his boundless mission: "Therefore go and make disciples of all nations" (Matthew 28:19). God's un-merited love received by his disciples must now be relayed to every people group on the planet. It's what disciples do.

But how? When the Spirit of Jesus begins to live in us, we take on his heart of compassion for those who have lost their way. We can no longer sit back and watch while people drift far from God, feeling abandoned and un-loved. That's not an option anymore. Love compels us to do something about it—perhaps something we've never done before.

For Jesus, that meant hanging out with people who had been left out. A tax collector named Matthew is a perfect example.

In Jesus' day, tax collectors were local Jewish men greedy for gain. Em-ployed by the Roman occupying force, they were notorious for charging too much, scraping the extra off the top, and lining their own pockets while Rome looked the other way.

Their peers saw them as traitors to their nation and thieves who would cheat innocent people to make themselves rich. Becoming friends with a tax collector was unthinkable. They were so despised, you wouldn't even want to be seen with one. Unless, of course, you are Jesus.

---

10.   John 10:10

11.   Ortberg, John, *Steps: A Guide to Transforming Your Life When Willpower Isn't Enough*, Carol Stream, IL: Tyndale House Publishers, 2025, p. 60.

By this point, Matthew had grown used to the snubs and dirty looks from every passerby. When Jesus invited him to be his disciple, he couldn't believe it! For the first time in his life, Matthew felt accepted and loved just for who he was. The experience deeply changed him. Soon after, a dilemma arose in his heart.

"This is so incredible," he must have thought. "I never knew someone like me, who has gone down so many wrong paths, could ever be loved and wanted by God." Then it hit him. "But what about my friends?"

Matthew knew firsthand the shunning and rejection his tax collector friends felt from their own people. He thought, "They might never come to hear Jesus teach in public. They're too afraid of how the crowd might treat them. How will I ever connect them with Jesus?"

Suddenly, an idea popped into his head: *throw a party!*

"That's it!" he thought. "My friends *love* a dinner party. I'll invite them and all the people that hang out with them. I'll also invite Jesus and his other disciples. When they all get in the same room, who knows what God might do?"

No one knew if this plan would work, but to everyone's surprise, it was a big hit. Of course, not everybody was crazy about the idea.

> *But when the Pharisees saw this, they asked his disciples, "Why does your teacher eat with such scum?"*
>
> —*Matthew 9:11 NLT*

You might wonder, "Why were these religious people so mean?" Next time you're in a group of four or more, have everyone say "grumble, grumble, grumble" for 10 seconds straight.

That's what pharisees sound like. They grumble. They complain. They have the spiritual gift of criticism. In general, they are angry, bitter, self-righteous, and proud. I know because I've been a pharisee along the way. They are everywhere, but they are not the only group in this story.

In Jesus' day, there were two kinds of people: the orthodox people like the Pharisees, who rigidly kept all 613 Jewish laws in the Bible, and those who did not keep the laws strictly if at all.

The second group was called "the people of the land." It was forbidden for the orthodox to go on a journey with the people of the land, to do any business with them, to give anything to them or receive anything from them, or to entertain them as guests or be guests in their homes.

By eating with people like this, Jesus was doing something the pious people of his day would have never done. Their concern was to keep themselves holy before God. Jesus' concern was to help people find their way back to God. Their approaches were diametrically opposite. Which would you choose?

In fact, when the religious leaders had it up to their eyeballs with Jesus, they said, "You…you're just a glutton, a drunkard. Why…*you are a friend of sinners!*" It was the worst insult they could throw at him.

In effect, Jesus said, "Guilty." About his new friends, he replied,

> *"Healthy people don't need a doctor—sick people do."*
>
> —*Matthew 9:12 NLT*

A Friend of Sinners

If this is how the Great Physician heals people who are far from God, how can we as disciples of Jesus become friends of sinners, too?

- **First, *offer* God's grace**

A four year-old girl woke up one night frightened, convinced that in the darkness around her there were all kinds of spooks and monsters. Alone, she ran to her parents' bedroom. Her mother calmed her down and, taking her by the hand, led her back to her own room, where she put on a light and reassured her with these words: "You needn't be afraid. You are not alone here. God is in the room with you."

The girl replied, "I know that God is here, but I need someone in this room with skin on."[12]

God knew this too. Real love is being there in the flesh. In a world racked with fear and loneliness, Jesus' birth ushered in a revolutionary concept: God with skin on, the very presence of God in a person. When Jesus left heaven and came to earth, he modeled what grace-filled love looks like.

Leaving our world and entering someone else's is a profound way to offer God's grace. When we come across people who are dealing with a broken

---

12.   Scazzero, Peter, Warren Bird, and Ronald Rolheiser, *The Emotionally Healthy Church: A Strategy for Discipleship that Actually Changes Lives*, Grand Rapids, MI, South Barrington, IL: Zondervan ; Willow Creek Resources, 2015, p. 175.

dream, untamed fears, a lack of direction, or a sense of loneliness, what they need most is for someone to be there, in the room, with skin on.

A while back, I met with a promising young man who was really struggling. Deep down, he was angry. You could see it in the way he blew off his studies, treated his family, and spoke to his teachers. I had no idea what was troubling him, so I took a shot in the dark. "Have you lost anyone close to you?"

With his head down, he said slowly, "Yeah, my brother." He shared his devastation over his brother's death. Although it had been several years, he had looked up to his brother so much and still missed him every day.

After a while, I asked, "Are there other losses?"

He said, "Yeah, my grandma." She had died about three years before our conversation. For a moment, his face lit up when he talked about her, but losing her only fueled his sense of confusion, hurt, and anger.

To lighten the mood, I said, "Tell me about your dad. Where is he?"

"In jail," he answered.

After a pause, I asked, "How long has he been there?"

"Pretty much my whole life."

At that point, I knew I was leaving my world and entering his because I started to feel his grief. I began to understand where his anger came from—loss after loss after loss, all of them beyond his control.

We talked for a while longer and then set up another time. Considering all that he carried, I could have talked about the love of God for weeks on end and never made a dent. What this young man needed was someone with skin on. Someone who would enter his world and listen. Someone who would be with him.

Jesus' beloved disciple John wrote:

We love because he first loved us.

—1 John 4:19 NRSVUE

Jesus demonstrated God's love for us by personally entering our world. When we do that for others, we are offering grace.

- **Second, practice *acceptance* without approval**

This is a hard one. While traveling with one of my kids' sports teams, I found myself in a room one night with several other guys shooting the breeze. One of the other dads began sharing sports stories, telling off color jokes, and using some offensive language while drinking a few beers. He was entertaining, to be sure, even though I couldn't agree with several things he said.

The next day, another dad came to me privately. He knew I was a pastor and wondered what I thought about some of the behavior from the night before. I said in effect, "I don't expect someone who is not a Christian to act like one. Mark is a good guy who is far from God. He needs someone to accept him as he is. I don't have to approve of everything he says or does to do that."

Contrary to popular opinion, acceptance and approval are two different issues in a relationship. We can accept people without approving of their every action or belief. In fact, we do it all the time. We accept people in our family and friend circles who hold beliefs we don't agree with, promote political positions we oppose, or engage in behaviors we find annoying or destructive. Is there any marriage where both people approve of everything their partner says and does? (If so, I want to meet them!) What parent-child relationship enjoys total approval of all things said and done by both parties? In most cases, these differences don't keep us from accepting others, even if we wish their way of life was more like ours.

Acceptance has been a fundamental part of the Christian faith for two millennia. In what was likely a multi-cultural church with a variety of beliefs and behaviors, Paul instructed the early Christians in Rome to follow Jesus' example.

> *Accept one another, then, just as Christ accepted you, in order to bring praise to God.*
>
> *—Romans 15:7*

How did Christ accept you? Fully, lovingly, and with no strings attached. When we accept others this way, it brings praise to God because it shows God's heart of love for all people.

Thankfully, Jesus did not make approval of our behavior the starting point of his relationship with you or me. If he had, there would be no relationship—ever.

Jesus didn't approve of our sin; he died for it. Paul put it this way: "But God demonstrates his own love for us in this: While we were still sinners, Christ died for us."[13]

---

13. Romans 5:8

By his death and resurrection, Jesus defeated sin and death. His victory removed the sin barrier that separated us from a real relationship with God. As a result, he can meet us exactly where we are and say:

"Have you ever lied to cover your tracks, said things to hurt people, or acted selfishly, which caused others harm? If so, I died to free you from that.

"What about turning your back on God? Have you ridiculed people of faith while keeping dark secrets about your own behavior? Is there some heinous act you have committed? I took that on the cross, too.

"Is an addiction destroying your life and relationships? Does lust consume your thoughts? Do deep hurts keep you trapped in bitterness? My wounds can heal yours.

"If, over time, you have become weary of carrying these burdens, come to me, and I will give you rest. There is nothing you have thought, said, or done that my sacrifice on the cross cannot cover. I accept you fully. Come as you are. I love you."

This is the gospel of Jesus. The starting point of his relationship with us is total acceptance without approval. It is the essence of love. Few of us struggle to accept others who meet our approval. The real test lies in accepting those whose thoughts, words, or actions conflict with our own. Until we learn to love this way, we will find it hard to be "a friend of sinners."

Time and again, Jesus showed us that the seed of change can only take root in the rich soil of acceptance. To witness true transformation in others, we must first embrace them fully—just as they are.

- **Third, *acknowledge* God at work**

At this very moment, there are things God is doing in your life and mine that we can't see. For months, my wife struggled at her job. She prayed, she cried, she talked with co-workers and supervisors, friends and spiritual advisors, all to no avail. The basic issues at her work refused to change. Finally, one Friday afternoon, she hit a breaking point. On her commute home, she cried out to God, "I've done everything I possibly can, Lord. This isn't changing, and I just can't bear it any longer. If this is your will, I ask you to open a job in my field right in our city."

Early the next morning, she opened her email and saw a listing for her dream job. She applied, interviewed, and received a job offer, all in two weeks. It came with an increase in pay and vacation time, and it was just 10 minutes from our house.

Did that job suddenly open in the roughly 12 hours between her prayer and seeing the email? Nope. The process was much longer. What my wife didn't know during those months of frustration and sleepless nights was how God was shifting and aligning things just so. She couldn't see it, but God had been working on her behalf all along.

God is always at work before we recognize it. The theological term for this experience is prevenient grace. It is the grace of God that goes before us, working in us and others before we are even aware of it and drawing us toward God.

When God sent Jesus into the world, it was part of a much larger plan that we couldn't see.

> *...that God was reconciling the world to himself in Christ,*
> *not counting people's sins against them. And he has committed to us*
> *the message of reconciliation.*
>
> —*2 Corinthians 5:19*

God's reconciling work started long before we came on the scene and continues to this day. As a result of Christ's work on the cross, God is not counting people's sins against them. God is about reconciliation not retribution. Like a father running out to hug his long-lost child, God aches to see every wayward child come home. This is the unmerited love of God.

As disciples, we both receive and relay this grace. We have been appointed as ambassadors of God's reconciling love shown in Jesus Christ, but we are never the first ones on the scene. When we go to someone in need or talk with someone who is confused or doubting, we don't *bring* God into the room. God is already there. We're the latecomers to the party.

Imagine how our conversations might change if we were humble enough to freely offer someone unmerited love, accept that person without blanket approval, and acknowledge that God is already at work in his or her life?

Talk about life changing! And not a minute too soon. Not long ago, a survey by the Barna Group found that 70 percent of Americans will never set foot inside a church. Of course, they may come if it's required for a wedding or a funeral, but voluntarily, they are not walking through a church door.

How will 70 percent of the US population ever taste the grace of God? The internet has been an effective tool for reaching some, but generally, it only serves those searching for Christian content.

A far more effective way to distribute the grace of God is Jesus' method: become "a friend of sinners." Love people the way he did. Maybe we could throw a "Matthew Party" where we invite our non-churched friends to rub shoulders with some of our Christian friends. Who knows what kind of spiritual sparks might fly?

A backyard BBQ, a board game night, a night at the ballpark, or a simple book club could lay the foundation for relational bridges to form. We don't have to agree with people or approve of everything they do to love them. Jesus certainly didn't. Instead, he made hanging out with those who were left out his mission.

For I have come to call not those who think they are righteous, but those who know they are sinners.

—Matthew 9:13 NLT

To be honest, I'm so glad Jesus is a friend of sinners. Otherwise, I wouldn't know him. Now, I want all my friends to know him. Maybe you do, too.

CHAPTER THREE

Life Together

The most terrible poverty is loneliness and the feeling of being unloved.

—Mother Teresa

I've been lonely for years, but I never realized it until college when I lost my small group of close friends and couldn't make more. Eventually I met my wife, we had kids, and I got through school and got a good job. I always thought that would fix my loneliness, but it never did. While I'm surrounded by people, I'm isolated.

—Jacob, Age 30[1]

It's a subject still taboo in most quarters. Jacob unmasked his quiet desperation on a site dedicated to breaking the silence. Notably, he was not reaching out to connect with anyone. There is no way to trace his story back. He simply felt the need to share his inner isolation on the off chance it might ease his pain. Jacob never dreamed life would be like this. He ended his post with a confession, "I thought I wasn't lonely for a long time, but recently I realized I'm lonelier than ever."[2]

He's not alone. According to the US Surgeon General, America is facing an epidemic of loneliness. The stats are sobering. One in two US adults report feelings of loneliness with some of the highest rates among young adults.

1.　Korda, Colin Rumball & Marissa, The Loneliness Project, Accessed October 14, 2024, https://www.thelonelinessproject.org/?a=283.

2.　Ibid.

More than just a bad feeling, loneliness places us in mortal danger. In his advisory to the nation, the Surgeon General said, "Lacking social connection can increase the risk for premature death as much as smoking up to 15 cigarettes a day."[3]

Statistically, loneliness is also associated with other health consequences:

- A 29% increased risk of heart disease
- A 32% increased risk of stroke
- Increased incidents of depression and dementia[4]

These harsh physical realities are only part of the story. On the economic front, absenteeism fueled by loneliness costs US employers an estimated $154 billion annually.[5]

Something has gone terribly wrong. We live in an age of interconnectedness that was unimaginable a generation ago, yet we are lonelier than ever. Social media once promised it would cure isolation, but research tells a different story: the more connected we are online, the more disconnected we feel inside.

What's missing? Clearly the most important earthly ingredient to happiness—and it is all around us.

The Key to Happiness

"The pursuit of happiness" has long been part of the American psyche, but it arises from a much deeper impulse in the human heart. We have sought humanity's holy grail in a wide variety of forms: freedom, wealth, power, security, achievement, health, enlightenment, and purpose to name a few. What if the key to happiness is much simpler?

In their book, *The Good Life*, authors Robert Waldinger and Marc Schulz reveal the findings of the world's longest scientific study of happiness. For 85 years, the Harvard Study of Adult Development tracked the lives of thousands of people. After drilling down through mountains of data collected across three generations, here's their bedrock conclusion:

---

3. HHS/OASH, *Our Epidemic of Loneliness and Isolation*, April 25, 2023, p. 8. https://www.hhs.gov/sites/default/files/surgeon-general-social-connection-advisory.pdf.

4. Ibid.

5. Ibid., pp. 8–9

> *Positive relationships are essential to human well-being.*[6]

Waldinger fleshed out their findings this way:

> *The people who were happiest, who stayed healthiest as they grew old, and who lived the longest were the people who had the warmest connections with other people.*[7]

Happiness is all about *relationships*. This longest-ever study of adult development found that positive relationships are more important to our well-being than money, status, achievement, health, or geographic location. In fact, without positive relationships, we will find other connections to fill the void.

Journalist Denby Fawcett wrote about a group of gang members showing up at the state legislature in Hawaii. They came seeking funding for a nonprofit that could free them from lives of petty crime. When a lawmaker asked one of the teens what led him to join a gang, he said, "To be known."[8]

We get that. It's a longing in our hearts, too. Although you and I may not have met or connected in any way, I know one of your greatest needs. It's the same as mine. We need to be understood—to be known and accepted for who we are. Without that, every person we see reminds us of how alone we feel.

Created for Community

Our deep need for relationships springs from an even deeper well. From the very beginning, we were created for community.

As God went about creating human beings in the second chapter of Genesis, a curious fact soon arose about the first man. Adam was set in a beautiful garden with all his needs abundantly supplied. God gave him purposeful work to care for the garden, and Adam lived in perfect relationship with God and all creation. Yet, he was lonely.

---

6. Waldinger, Robert J. and Marc S. Schulz, *The Good Life: Lessons from the World's Longest Scientific Study of Happiness*, New York: Simon & Schuster, 2023, p. 29.

7. Liebergall, Molly and Robert J. Waldinger, "Author Talks: The World's Longest Study of Adult Development Finds the Key to Happy Living," McKinsey & Company, February 16, 2023. https://www.mckinsey.com/featured-insights/mckinsey-on-books/author-talks-the-worlds-longest-study-of-adult-development-finds-the-key-to-happy-living.

8. Fawcett, Denby, "Denby Fawcett: The Lonely Backgrounds that Trigger Mass Shooters," Honolulu Civil Beat, July 12, 2022. https://www.civilbeat.org/2022/07/denby-fawcett-the-lonely-backgrounds-that-trigger-mass-shooters/.

Nothing like this had ever happened. In all the creative work God had done, everything was good—*very good*. But the moment God saw Adam's condition, God said, "*Not* good." Something had to be done.

> *Then the LORD God said, "It is not good that the man should be alone; I will make him a helper as a partner."*
>
> —*Genesis 2:18 NRSVUE*

In this unfolding story, notice when Adam's loneliness occurs. It is before sin enters the world. In other words, it is not our disobedience to God, dedication to ourselves, or disregard for creation that make us lonely. None of those factors existed at this point. Adam enjoyed perfect union with God and creation and had everything he could possibly need—except a partner.

Out of love, God put the man into a deep sleep, took one of his ribs, and created a woman. When God placed her before the man, Adam did what every man does when he first casts his eyes on a woman in all her created glory. He broke into poetry.

> *This at last is bone of my bones*
> *and flesh of my flesh;*
> *she shall be called Woman,*
> *because she was taken out of Man.*
>
> —*Genesis 2:23 RSV*

Can you feel the deep connection? They were literally made for each other. Finally, in this relationship, they could both know and be known, love and be loved, as equals. A crucial part of God's good creation is our need for companionship. We can't thrive without it.

Young children know this. After being laid off, a friend took a job out of state. For weeks at a time, he was away from his family. When he came home, his two young daughters simply clung to him. It's not that they wouldn't let him out of their sight; they wouldn't let him out of their grasp—for hours on end! They knew it was not good for them—or him—to be alone.

Something in us physically aches for relationship. Over time, isolation changes our blood chemistry, affects vital organs, and leads to serious illness or even an early grave. It's not just the emotional low of a lonely heart. Loneliness touches us on a cellular level. But it goes deeper than that.

Basic Building Block

It's a question as old as wonder itself: what are the smallest pieces that make up all things? The ancients identified four basic elements: earth, sky, fire, and water. Minds in the Middle Ages proposed sulfur, mercury, and salt. By the 19th century, scientists were sure the basic building blocks for all things were atoms.

However, as technology advanced, we found that atoms are made up of smaller things: protons, neutrons, and electrons. That solved the issue until we discovered that protons and neutrons were made of something smaller: quarks. In recent years, scientists have identified even smaller particles called neutrinos and photons.

But post-Einstein quantum physics asserts there is a more basic building block than atoms and all their sub-atomic particles: relationships.

Physicists found these sub-atomic particles aren't even visible until they are in relationship with other particles. In effect, relationships bring them into being and hold them together. The entire universe is composed of "bundles of potentiality" that only display their potential in a relationship.[9]

No wonder our bodies react so severely to loneliness. At our core lies a vast potential, revealed only in communion with others. It's how God made the heavens and the earth.

Somehow, Paul knew this. Long before quantum physics, he shared this deep insight about Jesus with the early Christians in Colossae:

> *He is the image of the invisible God, the firstborn of all creation, for in him all things in heaven and on earth were created, things visible and invisible…He himself is before all things, and in him all things hold together.*
>
> —*Colossians 1:15–17 NRSVUE*

The Deepest Level

Finally, we come to the deepest level. We are not only created for relationships; we are created from them. The one eternal God, Creator of the universe, exists in a beautiful community of the Father, the Son, and the Holy Spirit. Their mutual love for each other is so pure, their union so perfect, that

---

9. Wheatley, Margaret J., *Relationships: The Basic Building Blocks of Life*, 2014. https://margaret-wheatley.com/wp-content/uploads/2014/12/Relationships-The-Basic-Building-Blocks-of-Life.pdf.

they are called the three in One, the Trinity, the Triune God. Jesus described it this way: "the Father is in me, and I in the Father" (John 10:38).

Community is the very image of God stamped on our souls. It is not just that relationship holds our bodies together at a sub-atomic level.

Our need for relationships is soul-ular.

Formed for God's Family

From the beginning, we were formed for God's family. Here's how the Apostle Paul describes it:

God decided in advance to adopt us into his own family by bringing us to himself through Jesus Christ. This is what he wanted to do, and it gave him great pleasure.

—Ephesians 1:5 NLT

Adoption is life changing for all involved. Over the years, I've known many people who have adopted children, some within this country and some internationally. What brings tears to my eyes is the joy on those parents' faces when they bring their children home for the first time. It is inexpressible. When God adopts us into his family through Jesus, that is precisely the kind of pleasure we give our heavenly Father.

All this comes out of love. Jesus' life, death, and resurrection were God's plan to forgive us of our wrongdoing, deliver us from evil, offer us a new life in the Spirit, and adopt us into a family to help restore the image of God in us. The lover of our souls knew from the start it was not good for humans to be alone. That's why the Psalmist says,

God sets the lonely in families.

—Psalm 68:6

I was set in a faith family soon after I was born. My early understanding of the family of God revolved around the large group of people who gathered each Sunday. As a kid, I endured the sermons by playing tic tac toe on the bulletin with my mom or sliding under the pews and popping up in another row to give some elderly lady a near coronary. I also attended age-appropriate Sunday school classes. In both cases, the focus was on cognitive learning. Still, there was a sense of being part of something bigger, and I knew people cared about me.

At age 14, at the urging of my high school Sunday school teacher, Sharon Rust, I invited Jesus into my heart. It was a powerful spiritual encounter that changed everything. Suddenly, being part of the family had a personal dimension to it. Practicing my faith was not just about showing up on Sunday morning, it involved reading the Bible on my own and taking stabs at prayer.

For years, I thought this interplay of weekly worship and daily devotion was the ultimate way to follow Jesus. Sadly, I was mistaken. While these are good practices that I still follow today, by themselves they never dealt with the deeper issues in my life. Personal problems remained unsolved, harmful patterns went unaddressed, and destructive habits were left unchecked. I never let someone get close enough to speak into my life. Frankly, I didn't know what I was missing.

Two Out of Three Ain't Good

Somehow, I had never learned the three contexts for experiencing God. Large group and personal devotion I had already established. What I needed was the power of a small group. Ironically, multiple examples in Scripture were hiding in plain sight.

All through the Gospels, we see Jesus teach large crowds, often numbering in the thousands, but he spent most of his time with a small group of 12 disciples. There he taught, mentored, and did life together with his closest followers. In fact, he shared even deeper things with the small executive team of Peter, James, and John.

In the second chapter of Acts, tongues of fire representing the Holy Spirit came upon the disciples and others in an upper room in Jerusalem. These once fearful, dejected disciples were suddenly filled and empowered by the Holy Spirit. When Peter stood up and preached about Jesus and the resurrection to a bewildered crowd, three thousand people surrendered their lives to Christ. The scene culminates with a snapshot of what the earliest Christian community looked like.

They devoted themselves to the apostles' teaching and to fellowship, to the breaking of bread and to prayer... Every day they continued to meet together in the temple courts. They broke bread in their homes and ate

together with glad and sincere hearts…And the Lord added to their
number daily those who were being saved.

—Acts 2:42, 46–47

It's God's original blueprint for the church. Day by day, these freshly minted followers met together in the temple courts (large group) and in their homes (small group). It became such a well-established pattern that decades later when the Apostle Paul was bidding farewell to the church in Ephesus, he left the elders with these words in Acts 20:20 (CEB), "You know I held back nothing that would be helpful so that I could proclaim to you and teach you both publicly and privately in your homes." This large group/small group design has been called God's 20/20 vision for the church.

But it doesn't end in the book of Acts. Multiple times in his letters, Paul encouraged his readers to greet the churches that met in various disciples' homes.[10]

Small groups were a big part of what it meant to follow Jesus in the early church because they were crucial to growing disciples and leaders. As the third of our six "G's," deeply devoted disciples intentionally do life together with a few other people. Here's what it means to engage in a group:

A disciple regularly connects with a handful of other disciples to taste grace,
apply Scripture, and together encourage one another to become like Christ
in thought, word, and action.

Small groups offer a unique environment for experiencing God that a large group and personal devotion simply cannot provide. Let's look at their respective benefits.

Large Group:

Gathering with dozens, hundreds, or thousands of people at a time brings energy and momentum. It gives us a sense that we're part of something bigger—a movement that's changing our lives. These settings are designed to experience inspiration and gain a sense of the greatness of God. When gathered in a large group, there is often a call to make a personal decision that will alter the direction of our lives. However, by design, only a few designated

---

10.   See Lydia (Acts 16:40), Priscilla and Aquila (Romans 16:3–5, 1 Corinthians 16:19), Nympha (Colossians 4:15), and Apphia and Archippus (Philemon 1:2).

people can speak, typically those with special training. The vast majority are there to listen and respond as led by the Spirit.

Small Group:

Small groups are a very different experience. They usually consist of three to twelve people in a home, workplace, or restaurant who meet two to four times a month. The intentionally smaller size gives the group a family feel. Openness is encouraged, and over time, people build enough trust to pull down the mask and say, "Look, I know the image I project, but underneath, here's who I really am." Real relationships like this foster spiritual intimacy where people can know and be known, love and be loved.

Small groups are a pathway to the closeness of God. Contrary to a larger gathering, a small group is more about process than decision. Hanging out with a handful of people gives us space and supportive friends to turn our decisions into daily actions that transform us. Finally, with fewer people, there is no monologue by a professional Christian. Small groups are an "All Play." Everyone gets to talk, and everyone has an opportunity to serve and pray for others.

Personal Devotion:

Our one-on-one relationship with God reveals our status as a child of God and a person of worth. Time alone with God opens the door in the chapel of our heart to the indwelling presence of the Holy Spirit. In describing Jesus, the prophet Isaiah said, "A bruised reed he will not break, and a smoldering wick he will not snuff out" (Isaiah 42:3). In times of brokenness and grief, it's his tenderness that leads us to deeper surrender. As we sit in the quiet, we discover a high priest whose tender mercy binds our wounds and heals our soul.

In short, the three contexts look like this.

Large Group	Small Group	Personal Devotion
Movement	Family	Child of God
Inspiration	Intimacy	Indwelling
Greatness of God	Closeness of God	Tenderness of God
Life Decision	Life Process	Life Surrendered
Priesthood of Few	Priesthood of All	Jesus my High Priest

Again, large group and personal devotion are crucial practices of a fol-lower of Jesus. They still sustain me today. But two out of three aren't good for a deeply devoted disciple. Until I found a small group, I lost out on one of the greatest benefits of becoming a part of God's family—authentic community.

Launching Community

Unfortunately, launching this kind of community is no easy task. We get inspired by the early believers devoting themselves to the Apostle's teaching and to fellowship and think, "That's what we need to do. Let's have a potluck dinner!" Not the same.

For many Christians, "fellowship" has devolved to clutching a cup of coffee, eating a doughnut, and talking about our favorite sports team in the "fellowship hall." It's nice, but we're still missing what Jesus' first followers experienced.

On a deeper level, here are some common behaviors that undermine true community:

- Wearing a game face that pretends everything is alright when it is not
- Shallow politeness that vies for favor or position
- Tip toeing around people to avoid triggering them
- An unwillingness to admit to or deal with loss and grief
- An inability to say "I was wrong" or "I'm sorry"
- Seeing every suggestion as a personal attack or rejection
- Choosing to play a role rather than enter into someone's deep need
- Saying "yes" when everything in us wants to say "no"
- A relentless busyness that blocks us from unhurried time with God, others, or ourselves

Most of us have been in fractured families, friendships, marriages, work-places, or church groups where some of these behaviors are in play. None of us would confuse that experience with authentic community. Our body and soul crave so much more. What if those relationships could be different?

Spoiler alert: they can! But not without some re-wiring. What is missing in so many instances is trust-filled, accountable relationships. At the center of our soul is a longing for three ways of being to converge: loving, deep, and truthful. First up is loving.

Loving

Many of us feel stuck. Our job no longer brings life. Our friendships feel stale. It feels like our dating life is going nowhere, or we find our marriage in a holding pattern. We can't lose the weight we don't want or say no to an addictive behavior that is pulling us under.

We've tried to make changes. Really, we have. But none of them last. What are we missing?

In a word, love.

Love is the precursor to transformation. Ironically, we can only change when we feel fully accepted as we are. When we try to make changes out of guilt or shame, they always snap back on us. We end up doing more of the very thing we wanted to do less.

As mentioned in the last chapter, Paul described this dilemma in his letter to the early Christians in Rome:

"The desire to do good is inside of me, but I can't do it. I don't do the good that I want to do, but I do the evil that I don't want to do."

—Romans 7:18–19 CEB

To experience lasting change, we must accept who and where we are first. But how?

That's the gift of a loving community. There is no force more powerful or more life-changing than grace—complete, unmerited love. And often, the place we experience it first is in a small group where we risk sharing the real stuff.

I remember the first time I shared some really awful things about myself with a handful of other people—things that I thought would disqualify me from being loved and immediately make them reject me. To my surprise, they said, "We know just where you have been. We are glad you are here. Come back next week."

When we can see in the faces of a few other people that we are loved and accepted despite what we have done, who we have done it with, or where we have been, an amazing transformation begins to take place. Somewhere inside, it occurs to us, "If these people can know all this stuff about me and still accept me, maybe God can, too."

That opens the door for deep inner change. We are finally able to accept ourselves the way God has already accepted us, as a beloved child of infinite worth. All this is possible by the redeeming work of Jesus' death on the cross that forgives our sins and breaks the power of sin to enslave our future.

By faith in him, we receive a new identity as forgiven and free followers. Now, with the help of our group, we can make changes that stick.

The experience of Jesus' life-changing love also ignites in us a desire to love others the way he does. One night a woman new to her small group tearfully shared that she had been diagnosed with breast cancer and would need surgery. The group immediately rallied around her and prayed for her healing.

At their next gathering, all the women in the group showed up in pink shirts to show their support. A flurry of phone calls, texts, and home-cooked meals during her recovery demonstrated their love in practical ways. Her small group could have said, "That's too bad. Hope everything works out for you." Instead, they chose to love her and walk with her through a time of deep need. They became Jesus to her.

Love is the pattern our Savior set. Jesus made it crystal clear to his own small group:

> *Just as I have loved you, you should love each other. Your love for one another will prove to the world that you are my disciples.*
>
> *—John 13:35 NLT*

Here's the question for us: is our love for one another proving to the world that we are disciples of Jesus? That's all that really matters.

If you are wondering what it means to love others, Paul lines it out to the division-prone church in Corinth:

> *Love never gives up.*
> *Love cares more for others than for self.*
> *Love doesn't want what it doesn't have.*
> *Love doesn't strut,*
> *Doesn't have a swelled head,*
> *Doesn't force itself on others,*
> *Isn't always "me first,"*

> *Doesn't fly off the handle,*
> *Doesn't keep score of the sins of others,*
> *Doesn't revel when others grovel,*
> *Takes pleasure in the flowering of truth,*
> *Puts up with anything,*
> *Trusts God always,*
> *Always looks for the best,*
> *Never looks back,*
> *But keeps going to the end.*
>
> **—1 Corinthians 13:4–7 MSG**

Paul then adds,

> *Let love be your highest goal!*
>
> **—1 Corinthians 14:1a NLT**

Love is the supreme value of the Christian faith. A Jesus-inspired small group is an incubator of a love that transforms lives. Such groups care too much about one another to stay in the shallow end. They are willing to go deep.

Deep

When our kids were young, one of the games they loved to play was hide and seek. They especially liked it when Daddy counted, and they got to hide. At age four, our daughter, Jane, had her own twist on the game. I would go into a room and say, "Where is Janie? I wonder where she could be?"

Suddenly, a little voice would say, "Look under here! I'm right here!" For her, the fun wasn't in the hiding. It was in being found.

As we get older, we get confused about that. We keep playing hide and seek, but we shift the focus to the hiding part. Our older son, Zach, wanted to be the champion hider. We can relate. We all keep some part of ourselves hidden.

Surprisingly, the church is a great place to hide. We can come in with a big plastic smile, shake hands all around, grab a hot drink, and sway to the music. By all outward appearances, things look great.

But inside it feels like our world is falling apart. There is a hole in our soul big enough to drive a semi through. Silently, we say to ourselves, "It's a good thing nobody here knows what my life is really like." And there in plain view, we're hiding.

Some of us are living a double life. To most of the world, our life is what can be outwardly seen—the 10 percent of the iceberg that is above the surface. And part of it is. But we know 90 percent of who we are is below the waterline. When asked, we are quick to say, "It's all good," but those words often cover up things that are not. It was the 90 percent below the surface that sunk the Titanic.

Maybe it is an addiction to pornography or shopping online. It could be a hair-trigger temper that explodes on people in destructive ways. Maybe we can't stop eating more than our body needs or find ourselves drinking alone almost every night. Perhaps we are secretly wondering if life is worth living, and we're afraid to tell another living soul.

Whatever the case, we can't we can't let anyone else know. They would think less of us and surely pull away. We can't bear that, so we hide.

Thankfully, there is something else going on inside. Deep below our hidden life, there is a little voice saying, "I'm under here. I'm right here."

At the center of our soul, we want to be found. We don't want to hide. There is too much pain and isolation there. We were created for community. Our truest voice knows that.

We want to be known by someone we can trust, someone who will accept us and not judge us, someone who is willing to walk with us toward wholeness, someone who loves us regardless of our past.

That's how our relationships are intended to work when we follow Jesus. He invites us into loving union with himself and one another.

But it's no walk in the park to get there. It requires a kind of intimacy that may be uncomfortable at first. We must be willing to say, *Into-me-see. See my hopes, my dreams, my fears, and my foibles. I invite you to look inside my soul and truly know me.*

To be that honest is risky business. Someone may misunderstand us, judge us, or leave us. Spiritual writer John Ortberg, knows this fear intimately but has found an even deeper truth.

> *We can only be loved to the extent that we're known...*
> *The very accomplishments I think will earn me love keep people at a distance.*
> *The very weakness I'm afraid of allows people to come close.*
> *You can be impressive. You can be connected. You can't be both.*[11]

---

11. Ortberg, John, *Steps: A Guide to Transforming Your Life When Willpower Isn't Enough*, S.l.:

Which would you prefer? The only way I know to find the connection our souls crave is to gather with a few other Christ-followers and build deep trust. The Psalmist says,

Deep calls to deep…

—Psalm 42:7 NRSVUE

It is God's invitation to a fuller life. The truth is most of us don't need more relationships. We need deeper ones. That's where we rediscover what we once knew: the fun is not in the hiding; it's in being found.

What would it be like to stop pretending and, with child-like trust, speak from our hearts without fear of being judged or abandoned? Many of us have only dreamed of relationships like this. Day after day, we bob and weave through a relational maze of self-absorbed and shallow people whose only apparent concern is their agenda. To find a group of real people who are both "loving" and "deep" seems too good to be true, but it is not. In fact, a Jesus-inspired community has one more indispensable dimension. It is truthful.

Truthful

One of the fastest ways to kill community is to settle for fake fellowship. Growing up in Illinois, we called it "midwestern nice." Whatever it is called in your neck of the woods, it's the reason why so many of our relationships are marred by hidden hurts and slow burning anger. We are more committed to peace keeping than truth telling.

In Paul's letter to the church in Ephesus, he urgently encourages these first-generation Christians to "no longer be children" buffeted by false ideas about God and crafty schemes:

But speaking the truth in love, we must grow up in every way into him who is the head, into Christ,

—Ephesians 4:15 NRSVUE

A primary way we grow up in Christ is by speaking the truth in love to one another. Sadly, many of us grew up in a family or church culture that put a very high price on being nice. We were not to rock the boat, ask pointed

Tyndale House Publishers, 2025 p. 121.

questions, or bring up sensitive issues. We learned quickly what not to talk about to promote smooth relations. The goal was to keep the peace at any cost.

All of us have experienced this counterfeit peace at some point. It's the "walking-on-eggshells" feeling we have with certain people. We so desperately want to avoid conflict and are so afraid of saying something that might set a person off that we limit our conversation to safe, non-controversial topics—never sharing anything personal. It becomes an ESPN and the Weather Channel type of relationship. No relationship at all, really.

Here's how this might sound:

- I can't tell my husband how I really feel about his temper. He'll go berserk!

- If I say anything to my parents about what my friends are doing, they will never let me out of the house.

- One of the women in our group constantly speaks negatively about others in the church. When called on it, she laughs and says she was just kidding.

- I feel led to say something to a guy in our group about his drinking habits, but he will just shut me down and refuse to talk.

- My wife is a wonderful woman, but I can't stand her critical jabs. I've tried to tell her, but every time I bring it up, it gets worse.

When relationships get less and less truthful, they become less and less real.

Regardless, some of us would say, "I'm not going there. I would rather keep the peace any day." That's understandable. It can be painful, and the greatest motivator in life is to avoid pain.

But be aware of the consequences. It may appear that the choice is between keeping a false peace (no pain) or lovingly speaking the truth (great pain), but that's not how it works. If we do not engage in truth telling and settle for "pseudo community," we will love that relationship to death. It will be a slow, agonizing death that is drawn out over years until the last vestige of a relational bond evaporates. This explains why long-term marriages of 30 or 40 years "suddenly" end in divorce. They have been dying for decades.

When it comes to authentic community, there is no pain free option. Our choice is not no pain or great pain. It is positive pain or negative pain—pain that leads to life or pain that leads to death. We may find that speaking the truth in love brings pain in the short run, but it offers the hope of a deeper and more loving relationship. Peace keeping in order to hang on to what we have will only ensure we lose it in the end. There's no community without candor.

To the church in Galatia, Paul gave specific instructions about this sensitive subject:

> *Brothers and sisters, if a person is caught doing something wrong, you who are spiritual should restore someone like this with a spirit of gentleness. Watch out for yourselves so you won't be tempted too.*
>
> *—Galatians 6:1 CEB*

Paul understood the delicate nature of restoring someone who had gotten off track spiritually, but he also knew the importance of this work for true community to be maintained. Trust-filled, accountable relationships can be life savers.

To be honest, we all have a world-class spin doctor living in our heads. We can call wrong right—and right wrong—if it's to our advantage. Who we really are sits right behind our ear. It's in our blind spot. We can't see it, but those around us can. Similarly, those around us have blind spots they can't see, but we can. That's why we need a group we can trust. In those relationships, we can discover who we really are and lovingly hold each other accountable to who we want to become.

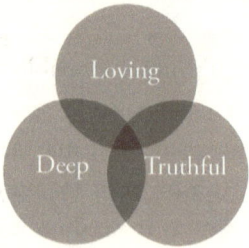

These three traits—loving, deep, and truthful—make up the relational core of authentic community. No two are enough.

Love and depth without truth leads to a pseudo community where bonds may run deep, but they are ripe for abuse. Many cults overwhelm people with love and encourage deep sharing, but without the truth of the gospel, they lead people down dark paths.

Loving and truthful community seems like a match made in heaven, but without deep sharing, they can skim across the surface and fail to deal with the issues that hold people in spiritual bondage.

Depth and truth can address the real issues in a person's life. But without the tenderness of love, precision is lost. Instead of a scalpel carefully removing sin, it feels like a sledgehammer to our soul. It hurts more than it helps.

In contrast, living in the center of all three is life giving! It brings joy, healing, and peace.

Of course, finding the center requires substantial effort. Some may wonder, "Isn't launching this kind of community time consuming?" No doubt. "Won't it be risky?" Absolutely. But we will never be satisfied with anything less. It's how God made us.

When we do life together in a group that's loving, deep, and truthful, the joyful result is real growth. Here are some identifiable signs of life change:

- We are less rushed and more loving.

- We have deeper compassion for the hurting and the poor.

- We are more grateful to God and less angry with others.

- We feel more at peace and more ourselves.

- We want to serve others.

- We exhibit more fruit of the Spirit described in Galatians 5:22–23.[12]

- Our relationships are better with our parents, spouse, kids, friends, classmates, co-workers, and neighbors.

- We laugh more.

- We forgive quicker.

- We are more open to racial reconciliation.

- We are more generous.

- If a friend had not seen us for a year, the difference would be noticeable.

---

12.   "But the fruit of the Spirit is love, joy, peace, forbearance, kindness, goodness, faithfulness, gentleness and self-control. Against such things there is no law" (Galatians 5:22–23).

What makes group life so deeply transformative? Jesus gives us a clue.

For where two or three gather in my name, there am I with them.

—Matthew 18:20

Maybe Jesus meant what he said, "where two or three gather...." Not two or three hundred or two or three thousand. Just two or three. A handful of people. In these small settings, Jesus shows up in a big way. Frankly, I will never forget the way Jesus showed up in Mary's group.

One Saturday night, I got one of those calls we all dread. Around 11:30, a panicked voice said, "Mary Manard is in the hospital, and she is dying."

Apparently, a few folks from Tim and Mary's small group had gone out for dinner and a movie that night. As they were coming out of the theater, Mary had a seizure. The ambulance rushed her to an emergency room. While there, she had a second seizure. Although they worked tirelessly and gave her the best medical treatment available, her life continued to ebb away.

A block away from the hospital, I received another call to say Mary had died. Like all who knew her, I was in shock.

Mary was 45 years old. She left a husband of nearly 20 years and three beautiful children, 16, 13, and almost 10 at the time.

Not long after I arrived at the hospital, Tim and I stood silently over the bed that held Mary's motionless body. Haltingly, we prayed together. It was a painfully real prayer with lots of tears. We were doing our best to process the unthinkable. For a few moments, Tim and I lingered in the room alone.

At one point, Tim said, "I am so glad this didn't happen three years ago. If it had, I don't know where she would be right now. But she has come so far in the last two to three years."

Surprised, I asked, "What made the difference, Tim?"

He immediately replied, "Our small group. We had both always believed in Jesus, but through our small group, we began to have a relationship with him. It made all the difference."

Later, he shared with me an email Mary wrote to their small group four months before she died. Since various people were moving away, the group had met the night before at Tim and Mary's house to share fond farewells.

Here's part of what she shared with her group:

Thank you all for being a part of our lives. For we know that no matter

*where each other goes, no matter what is going on in each of our lives good
or bad, whether we bring troubles from work, family, and personal life
to the gathering, we will always have a common bond that can never be
broken, as we all share the love and fellowship of God and his son Jesus and
that is something so awesome and spectacular!!! I can't begin to tell you how
much I smile and how it lifts my day when I think of spending eternity with
all of you one day!! I'll meet you at the gates with a glass of the beverage of
your choice and a party!*

Maybe Jesus was onto something. Perhaps following him is more caught than taught. We catch it not from a distance but when we are up close with a handful of people gathered in his name. In that space, Jesus shows up. He is with us.

Perhaps to save a really big world, it is best done in a small way. One by one, we enfold people into a little community and help them discover what they always hoped was true but never dared to believe.

Turns out, it's all about relationships.

Soul Food for the Long Run

The longest journey is the journey inwards.

—Dag Hammarskjöld

Ever known anyone who has lost everything?

In the late 2000s, I took my first trip to Liberia in West Africa. Ravaged by over a decade of civil war, the country was like nothing I had ever seen.

The people had lost virtually everything: family members, friends, homes, schools, and churches. The central power grid had been knocked out leaving most people without electricity or running water. Unemployment was officially at 90 percent.

Yet despite their horrific losses, the Christians I met in the many churches we visited had a joy and a richness of spirit that was contagious.

Coming back from that trip, I knew I needed to do something for my new friends but didn't know what. Suddenly, I got this crazy idea. What if I ran a marathon and asked people to sponsor me? The money could be used to start new churches, dig wells for clean water, and provide education for children who would otherwise never break the cycle of poverty.

There was just one problem. I had never run a marathon before. In fact, I hadn't been running for a couple of years, and I was in my late 40s. But I thought, "How hard could this be? You just keep running until the end."

As I began to train, God whispered, "Why don't you invite some others to do this with you?" Trusting that I wouldn't be laughed out of the building, one weekend in March, I stood up at the church I was serving in Springfield, Illinois and said, "I'm going to run the Chicago Marathon this fall to raise money for the precious people of Liberia. I just started my training last week. Who wants to run it with me? If you're interested, there's a sign-up sheet at the Welcome Center."

An audible gasp rippled through every service.

I thought I might get five or maybe eight people who would take me up on the idea. There were 33. Some of them were real marathoners. Others were novices like me. We met together from time to time, trained over the summer, and finally got to the big day in early October.

As I squeezed into the line with 35,000 of my closest friends, my heart was nearly beating out of my chest. All the people and the pageantry were enough to give anyone a rush.

But I was also nervous because I had never actually run a full marathon. All the training programs have runners do 20 miles as their longest run before they do it for real. Apparently, the adrenaline of race day is supposed to cover the rest.

That day I ran the best 15 miles of my life. To my surprise, it was fun. There were people lining the streets for miles cheering on this massive horde of everyday athletes. Many spectators held up homemade signs of encouragement. One placard said,

You Run Better than the Government!

At mile 15, I knew I had to take a break. After a brief walk around and some Gatorade, I started running again. It wasn't as smooth this time.

I hung in there for a while, but at mile 18, it suddenly felt like everything shut down. Anyone who has ever run a marathon knows that moment all too well. I had just hit the Wall.

The Wall is the point in the marathon when a runner's glycogen, the stored energy in the muscles, is depleted. This forces a runner to slow down the pace considerably, sometimes to a walk. It usually happens somewhere between mile 18 and 22. Unfortunately, a marathon is 26.2 miles.

To get to the finish line, I had to run through the Wall. It was the hardest part of the race. My legs felt like lead weights. I was fighting through pain with every step, and I still had eight miles to go! Everything in me wanted to quit.

Just then, somebody held up a sign with an egg-shaped guy sitting up high. It said,

Humpty Dumpty had wall issues too.

You don't have to run a marathon to have Wall issues. It's a predictable part of our spiritual journey as well. We hit the Wall when a crisis strikes. What happens next will deeply impact our faith life.

In their book, *The Critical Journey,* Janet Hagberg and Robert Guelich identify six stages of faith that lead to a deeper relationship with God. Each stage is intended to help us move forward in faith—if we allow it.

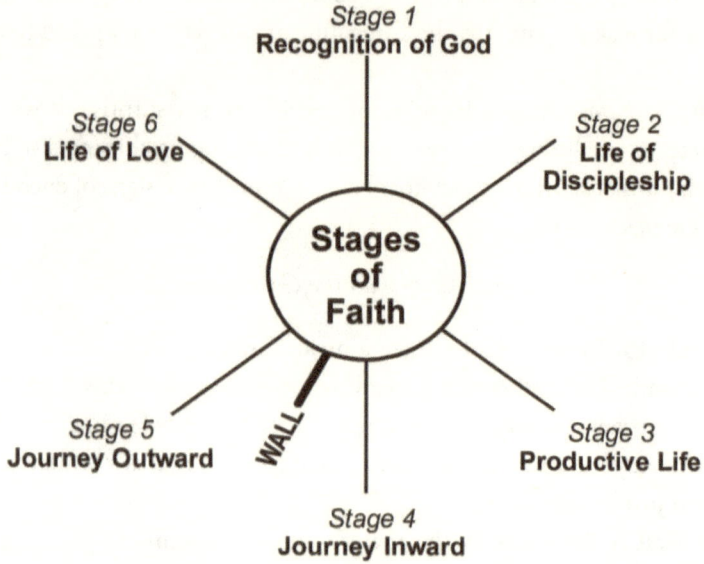

The Critical Journey
Stages in the Journey of Faith
by Janet O. Hagberg and Robert A. Guelich

Stage 1
Recognition of God

Stage 6
Life of Love

Stage 2
**Life of
Discipleship**

**Stages
of
Faith**

Stage 5
Journey Outward

WALL

Stage 3
Productive Life

Stage 4
Journey Inward

STAGE 1: The Recognition of God

Our journey with God begins with moments of awe and times of need. Awe dawns on us during profound experiences, such as witnessing a breathtaking landscape or the birth of a child. Although our early years are filled with wonder, awe tends to diminish with age due to rationalism and cynicism. Yet each time we are amazed, delighted, or loved unconditionally, it brings us face to face with something that transcends us. Awe is a doorway to recognize God as God. Scripture puts it this way: "the fear [awe] of the Lord is the beginning of knowledge."[1]

On the other hand, our need for God emerges through personal pain and unresolved circumstances. Guilt, rejection, dependency, anxiety, or a deep longing for something more drives us to seek solace in something greater than ourselves. In Jesus Christ, we find forgiveness and unmerited love, offering us a transformative new beginning and a new purpose for living. This experience of being loved by God just as we are, regardless of our past, marks a profound shift in our lives.

STAGE 2: The Life of Discipleship

Learning and belonging are the twin pillars of this stage. On our quest to discover more about God and what it means to follow Christ, we become apprentices who absorb as much as possible from more mature teachers and leaders. In a letter to early Christians in Corinth, Paul succinctly describes this process: "Be imitators of me, as I am of Christ".[2]

Much of our learning comes from doing life with others in a Christian community. Belonging to a group deepens our identity in Christ and encourages us to embrace spiritual disciplines that grow our faith such as prayer, Scripture study, Sabbath keeping, serving, and giving.

STAGE 3: The Productive Life

Now we enter the "doing" stage. Scripture says, "We love because [God] first loved us".[3] The immeasurable grace we've received in Jesus Christ propels us to witness and serve out of sheer gratitude. Building on our apprenticeship, we take responsibility to discover our unique gifts and talents and deploy them in service to Christ and others.

STAGE 4: The Journey Inward

1. Proverbs 1:7
2. 1 Corinthians 11:1 NRSVUE
3. 1 John 4:19

This stage throws a massive curve ball. An unforeseen crisis plunges us into questions and doubts we can't resolve. It may be a personal loss that strikes close to our heart: a family member, our health, or our livelihood is suddenly gone. In some situations, we may have a crisis of faith. Perhaps a revered and trusted leader falls from grace, and we're devastated.

Either way, for the first time, our faith doesn't work. The answers that had served us so well quicky turn into questions. Nothing feels certain anymore. We're hurt, confused, and angry. We think, "How could this happen? I've been so faithful." Like Jacob on his journey home in Genesis 32, we find ourselves locked in a wrestling match with God.

The Wall

That match signals our arrival at the Wall. Although it doesn't feel like it in the moment, the Wall is a crucial part of our healing and transformation. But what exactly is it?

As Hagberg and Guelich describe it, "The Wall represents our will meeting God's will face to face."[4] Before landing there, we never knew such a place existed. Sometimes the Wall leads us to the inward journey of faith. At other times, the inward journey leads us to the Wall. Either way, the Wall is where we wrestle with our will verses God's will in our lives.

Until this point, we have called all the shots. When we hit the Wall, we are invited to relinquish that right. Of course, we rarely do so without a fight. By our own gifts and strength, we try to climb the Wall, dig under it, go around it, or simply ignore it. In the end, however, none of those tactics work. The only way forward is through the Wall. When we are willing, God helps us dismantle it brick by brick. This slow process fosters the healing needed to move to the next stage.

STAGE 5: The Journey Outward

To our surprise, the Wall doesn't end our journey with God—it transforms it. We rediscover God not on our terms but as the God of the universe truly is. This time around we choose complete surrender to God's will, fully aware but not afraid of the consequences. The healing from our inner journey now motivates us to move outward and start "doing" again for God.

---

4. Ibid., p. 114

At first glance, this stage might look a lot like stage three, but this time, we serve and give out of a deeply poised center that treasures God's profound love for us.

STAGE 6: The Life of Love

By the time we reach stage six, nothing in our lives is about us anymore. Everything is about God. God's Spirit moves freely in us and through us for the sake of others. We are fully at peace with ourselves and with God and are willingly obedient to whatever God's call may be. By losing who we thought we were, we discover who we truly are. It's what John Wesley, the founder of Methodism, described as God's true goal for our lives: to be made perfect in love. "Perfect love casts out all fear,"[5] so Christ's pure love can shine through us toward others.

Talk about a journey! Let's drink it in for a moment. At first, it's tempting to think these stages follow a linear, stair-step progression, giving those in a higher stage greater status. Hagberg suggests a more apt metaphor is a circle. God is in the middle, and the people in each stage around its edge are equally valued and loved. We all have equal access to God, regardless of our current stage.[6]

As you consider the circle, where do you find yourself? Overachievers might be tempted to fast track this process and skip over the Wall part. Unfortunately, we don't have that option.

Just as we physically mature from birth through childhood to adulthood, each of these stages builds on the one before. We can't skip from stage three to six any more than we can skip from seven years-old to 47. However, unlike our physical nature, it is possible to get stuck in a stage or regress to a former one.

The Ordinary Way

Wherever we find ourselves now, these stages of faith give us a gift. They show us the path people of faith have been taking for centuries.

---

5.   1 John 4:18 NRSVUE

6.   Ibid., pp. xv–xvi

Over 500 years ago, St. John of the Cross wrote about Walls in his book, *Dark Night of the Soul.*

He explained the key to spiritual maturity this way: to move beyond the beginning stages of faith, we must receive God's gift of the dark night. He called this the "ordinary way" we grow in our life with God. Walls were certainly an ordinary feature for people in the Bible.

Abram faced a Wall when God promised to make him a great nation. He had to wait 25 years before his wife, Sarah, gave birth to their only child, Isaac.

Joseph faced a Wall when he was sold into slavery by his brothers and then unjustly thrown into a dungeon for up to 13 years—all through his late teens and 20s.

Esther faced a Wall when her husband, the King of Persia, ordered the extermination of the Jewish people throughout the land. She risked her life before the King to rescue her people.

However, in the Old Testament, the person with the greatest Wall issues was Job. Here's the scene described in Job 1:13–22. In the span of a few minutes, four messengers burst into Job's peaceful abode and breathlessly tell him tragic news.

The first one reported a raiding tribe that stole all his oxen and donkeys. While he was still speaking, the second told of how the fire of God fell from the heavens and burned up all his sheep and servants. While he was still speaking, the third messenger revealed how a different raiding tribe made off with his camels. In each case, all Job's servants were put to death save the messenger.

If that weren't enough, the final messenger's words pierced Job's heart. A mighty wind collapsed the house where his children were feasting, and all 10 of them died.

Shortly after losing his children and his wealth, Job also lost his health. He was struck with painful sores from head to foot. Except for his wife, he lost everything.

Nothing about it made sense. How could a good God allow such terrible things to happen to him, a man well known for his deep faithfulness? It was not right. It was not fair. In utter despair, he longed to die, "Why is light given to those in misery, and life to the bitter of soul?"[7]

Job had hit the Wall.

---

7. Job 3:20

Senseless

Sooner or later, we too are hit by a crisis that rocks our world. A close friend or family member dies. We lose our job. We go through a divorce. Suddenly, life doesn't make sense.

It may come as a betrayal, a broken dream, a bankruptcy, the loss of a child, a jail sentence, an accident, a heart attack, a bad church experience, an addiction, abuse of some kind, a loss of interest in spiritual things, infertility, or an errant child or grandchild. Any of these and hundreds of other turning points can bring us to our knees and make us question everything.

The Wall is not a respecter of persons. One Sunday, a pastor stood up at church and shared the heartbreaking story of his wife's sudden brain cancer. The time from her first headache on Thanksgiving Day to the moment she entered eternity was less than three weeks.

She left behind her husband and three grieving children. This pastor and his family had seen miraculous answers to prayer countless times in their lives, but when they prayed more fervently than ever for their beloved wife and mother, God was unexplainably silent. That's when their faith shut down.

He said, *"When you hit the Wall, what you believe and your life experience don't seem to match up."*

In those times, everything goes dark, and we start wondering out loud if we've just been fooling ourselves all along about this whole God thing.

Not the First Time

Truth be told, running a marathon was not the first time I had Wall issues. In a church I served, a staff member had a messy moral failing. When it came to light, it threw the congregation into a crisis. After an intense process, the staff member was released.

Unfortunately, it didn't end there. I was inwardly distraught over how the incident hurt the church. Even worse, I got caught up in the unfairness of it. The extra work piled on my plate because of someone else's sin embittered me, and I couldn't get over it. I kept saying to myself, "I don't deserve this."

Apart from my issues, the church needed a steady, calming presence to move through the mess, so I begrudgingly overworked to the point of exhaustion.

By sheer grace, I scheduled my first ever eight-day silent prayer retreat that summer. I drove to a retreat center out of state and met with my spiritual director. On day one, I framed it up for him like this: "Look, I'm done doing life this way. I'm not sure, but I may be done with ministry. My soul feels like scorched earth. I pray and get nothing. I read the Bible and don't hear God speak to me. I can't keep living like this. Something has to change.

"Here's what I do know. I'm going to stay married to Leanne, and I'm going to continue to be Zach and Jane's Dad. Other than that, everything is on the table."

My spiritual director rubbed his hands together and said, "Oh, this is wonderful! What a gift to start this retreat."

I said, "I don't think you caught what I was saying. This is *not* wonderful. There is nothing wonderful going on here. I am in agony. I feel dead inside. I don't know if I should be a pastor or a plumber. I have no idea which way I should go or what step I should take next. I feel lost."

With a gentle smile, he said, "Roger, God has you right where he wants you."

He knew what I didn't. God had me at the Wall.

Not Fun and Not Weird

Hitting a Wall is never a fun thing. It's painful and disorienting. We often feel abandoned and want to cry out like Jesus before he died, "My God, my God, why have you forsaken me?"[8] At the cross, even Jesus faced the Wall.

So many of us hit a Wall—some crisis that flips our world—and we go off the rails. Hurt and confused, we say, "See, this God stuff was never really true" and walk away from faith. It's an underlying reason why 40 million adult Americans who used to go to church stopped attending in the last 25 years.[9] Sadly, no one ever helped them see that the Wall is just the next step on their spiritual journey.

There's nothing wrong or weird about reaching a point where we feel like everything in us wants to quit God or the church. It is quite ordinary. We have simply reached the Wall. It's not there to punish us but to grow us. The Wall is an opportunity to become a deeper, more spiritually mature person.

---

8. Matthew 27:46; Mark 15:34

9. Davis, Jim, Collin Hansen, Michael S. Graham, and Ryan P. Burge, *The Great Dechurching: Who's Leaving, Why Are They Going, and What Will It Take to Bring Them Back?* Grand Rapids, MI: Zondervan Reflective, 2023, p. 3.

Of course, it's our choice. We can shrink back and camp out in stage two or three. We can bounce off the Wall, become bitter and shake an angry fist at God, or we can let God move us through the Wall to the other side. I wish someone would have explained this to me years ago.

Soul Food

If we choose to run through it, we will need some soul food to keep moving. The prophet Elijah learned this the hard way. Like Job, when Elijah hit his Wall, he just wanted to die.

After calling for a miraculous outpouring of God's power, deposing the prophets of Baal, and receiving a death threat from the wicked Queen Jezebel, Elijah lost all resolve. He walked a day's journey into the desert, sat down under a broom tree, and said, "It is enough; now, O LORD, take away my life."[10]

Hearing no response, he fell asleep. Suddenly, an angel touched him and urged him to eat. Next to his head was some baked bread and a jar of water. Elijah ate, drank, and went right back to sleep.

Undeterred, the messenger from God came a second time, offered more food and drink, and said, "Get up and eat, or the journey will be too much for you."[11] The double meal gave him strength to trek 40 days through the desert to Horeb, the mountain of God. There, God spoke to Elijah in a still, small voice, restored his hope, and gave him specific instructions for Israel's future. God had so much more for Elijah, but without that soul food, he never would have made the journey.

Elijah is not the only one. Running through a Wall takes a tremendous amount of energy. Yet we often do very little to feed our soul. Imagine doing a 20-mile march on half a bagel, every day, for months on end. At some point, we would collapse from lack of nutrition. It's no different in our spiritual lives.

Food Groups

None of us can make a long, hard spiritual journey without regularly taking in soul food. Some years ago, the US Food and Drug Administration released a food pyramid to illustrate the basic food groups necessary to hav-

---

10.   1 Kings 19:4 NRSVUE

11.   1 Kings 19:7 NRSVUE

ing a balanced diet. The right daily portions of food groups, such as grains, vegetables, fruits, and protein, will help us live a healthy life.

In the same way, a Soul Food Pyramid could help us live a healthy spiritual life. Although fried chicken, black-eyed peas, and collard greens may also nourish the soul, I'm referring to generous helpings of the G's.

In the first chapter, we talked about the soul food of God's glory. We can all establish a "Chapel of the Heart" to meet with God at any moment and all through the day. When we enter God's presence, we experience God's glory.

As we take in God's glory, it draws us to the table of grace. Apart from anything we have done, we receive God's unmerited love through Jesus Christ and relay that amazing grace to others.

The third soul food for a healthy diet is doing life in a group. In an increasingly lonely world, we reach out and connect with a handful of others to personally apply Scripture and encourage one another to become like Christ.

In this chapter, we add the fourth food group—growth. Here's what that means:

Deeply devoted disciples take personal responsibility for their spiritual journey by practicing spiritual disciplines that cultivate Christ-centered living and by helping others grow on their journey.

Don't be thrown off by the word discipline. In this context, we are not referring to punishment but rather practices that open our lives to love God and our neighbors. Engaging in certain practices is a key difference between Christians in name only and deeply devoted disciples. A common saying in the early church put it this way: "The soul and the body make a [person]; the spirit and discipline make a Christian."[12]

Spiritual disciplines come in a variety of forms, such as prayer, solitude, worship, fasting, service, and giving.[13] Yet, as valuable as they are, the disciplines themselves do not transform anyone. They simply put us in a receptive place where God can do the inner work needed to shape us into image bearers of Christ.

---

12. Wesley, John, *The Works of John Wesley*, Edited by Albert C. Outler, Vol. 4, Sermon 122, Abingdon Press, 1987, paragraph 7.

13. See Appendix A for a fuller listing of spiritual disciplines.

Powerful Predictor

With that goal in mind, one discipline rises above the rest as the single most powerful predictor of spiritual growth. Any guesses on which it is? Here's what the research shows.

In an extensive survey, Arnold Cole, Ed.D., and Pamela Caudill Ovwigho, Ph.D., polled 40,000 people ages eight to eighty to assess their level of engagement with the Bible. As they compiled the results, they made a surprising discovery.

Engaging with Scripture once or twice a week had little to no effect on key areas of a person's life. When someone's engagement increased to three times a week, there were small indicators of growth.

However, when a person reflected on Scripture four times a week, it led to a *huge* change in behavior. The survey uncovered nine key findings:

1. Loneliness drops 30%
2. Anger issues drop 32%
3. Bitterness in relationships drops 40%
4. Alcoholism drops 57%
5. Sex outside of marriage drops 68%
6. Feeling spiritually stagnant drops 60%
7. Viewing pornography drops 61%
8. Sharing one's faith jumps 200%
9. Discipling others jumps 230%[14]

These stunning stats reveal the transformative power Elijah and countless others have sought in their lives. Even now, imagine how many sincere and faithful people long to root out bitterness, overcome self-destructive behaviors, and triumph over temptations.

Why does regularly engaging with the Scriptures have this kind of impact on all ages? It's a primary way God speaks, and God's whisper gives us strength for the journey. Jesus says,

> *...the very words I have spoken to you are spirit and life.*
>
> —*John 6:63 NLT*

---

14. Martin, Jeff, "9 Tangible Benefits of Bible Reading for Your Church," Lifeway Research, January 20, 2021. https://research.lifeway.com/2021/01/20/9-tangible-benefits-of-bible-reading-for-your-church/.

Know the Truth

Do you know anybody who has trouble with his temper? Anyone who is paralyzed by her fear of financial ruin? How about a friend who tries but just can't seem to stop working, gambling, or playing video games? You probably know people who are hooked on internet pornography. They just haven't told you.

Someone may say, "Yes, of course, people get themselves into all kinds of desperate situations and compulsive behaviors. That's why we need to help people find their way back to God."

True, but I wasn't referring to pre-Christians. Certainly, when we disconnect from God, we are more prone to such struggles. It's the natural consequence of living life conformed to the values of this world.

However, when talking about people with unmanageable fears and compulsive behaviors, I was referring to those of us who count ourselves as Christians. We may have bowed the knee to Christ, have received his unmerited love and forgiveness, and sincerely desire to live our lives under his leadership, but we still find ourselves caught in destructive patterns. We may feel forgiven, but we don't feel free. Jesus explains this dilemma in a now famous phrase:

Then you will know the truth, and the truth will set you free.

—John 8:32

Jesus doesn't simply say the truth will set you free. We must know it first. As author Richard Foster put it, "Good feelings will not free us. Ecstatic experiences will not free us. Getting 'high on Jesus' will not free us. Without a knowledge of the truth, we will not be free."[15]

Self-Feeder

This kind of "freeing" knowledge requires deliberate action. When I received my M.O. (Masters of the Obvious), I noticed that most people eat every day. We feel hunger pains because our body is always burning calories, even while reading these words. Our spirit also burns energy continually—energy that needs to be replenished. To refill our spirit, we must learn a specific skill: self-feeding.

Like all parents, when our kids were very young, my wife and I had to spoon feed them. They were incapable of caring for their own nutrition. It was

---

15.   Foster, Richard J., *Celebration of Discipline: The Path to Spiritual Growth, Revised Edition*, New York: Harper & Row, 1988, p. 63.

sobering to me that they could be in a house full of food and starve to death if left on their own. They are young adults now, and thankfully, that's not a problem, but part of their growing-up process was to learn how to feed themselves.

The same is true in our spiritual lives. When we are infants in Christ, we need others to feed us. We haven't learned how yet. But to grow in Christ, we must become self-feeders. Here's why that's important.

Renewing Our Mind

Countless forces in this world are in a battle for our minds. Every day in the US, advertisers and influencers spend over a billion dollars to grab our attention. They bank on this fact: whatever captures our attention captures us. Perhaps that's why the Apostle Paul said,

> *Do not be conformed to this age, but be transformed by the renewing of the mind.*
>
> *—Romans 12:2 NRSVUE*

The best way to continually renew our minds is by reading and reflecting on Scripture. To help us gather the rich harvest of spiritual fruit in God's word, I use a REAP approach. It begins with a prayer:

"God, open the eyes of my heart to see, understand, and obey what You want to reveal to me in your Word today." I then engage with a passage of Scripture. REAP stands for:

R — Read. Read the passage twice. After the first reading, pause and reflect, then read again more slowly. It may help to read the passage out loud.

E — Evaluate. What is new to me from this reading? What did I learn about God? About myself? About the world or other people? Are there any commands to obey, principles to follow, or promises to enjoy?

A — Apply. Take two minutes in silent prayer. Set the stage by praying, "Holy Spirit, reveal how Your word is speaking to my real needs or the needs of others. Is there something specific You want me to do in response to this passage?" After listening in prayer, write down any word, phrase, image, or feeling that flashes in your mind or body, no matter how faint.

P — Pray. Write a prayer to God describing what has been revealed through this passage and ask for the power to follow the Holy Spirit's leading as soon as possible.

Imagine the spiritual growth that will take place day after day when we practice this simple discipline. To accelerate that growth, partner with one or two others to read through part or all of the Bible. Numerous reading plans exist on platforms like youversion.com and biblegateway.com to aid our Scripture engagement.

Many people take it to the next level by joining a long-term Bible study group that adds weekly teaching and discussion to daily readings.

Engaging with the Bible in these ways may be new ground for some, but a great harvest of blessing is promised to all who intentionally seek the Lord.

Plow new ground for yourselves, plant righteousness, and reap the blessings that your devotion to me will produce. It is time for you to turn to me, your LORD, and I will come and pour out blessings upon you.

—Hosea 10:12 GNT

Gifts Beyond the Wall

As we have seen, regularly feasting on this kind of soul food dramatically influences our behavior in healthy ways. But consuming large portions of soul food is so much more crucial when a crisis hits and life is spinning out of control.

In those times, the real question is, "Do we want to go through the Wall?" For some of us, the answer is no. We're so devastated we don't have the energy. In fact, we're not even sure it's possible. We would rather fall back into familiar patterns of discipleship and doing. Others of us are so mad over what has happened, we just want to quit God and the church and be left alone in our bitterness.

Still others, after the initial shock, want to take God to task. We can't believe God would allow such a horrible thing to happen, so we enter a wrestling match with the Almighty.

While wrestling at the Wall, a hidden truth comes to light. To get to the other side, something must be given up. It is different for each person, but typically it is part of our core self. We don't lose this element of our identity. Instead, after exhausting ourselves, we finally surrender it to God for God's purposes rather than our own.[16]

---

16.   Hagberg, Janet O. and Robert A. Guelich, *The Critical Journey: Stages in the Life of Faith, Second Edition*, Salem, WI: Sheffield Academic Press, 2005, p. 120.

This clears the way for us to run through the Wall. As we do, God offers us three transforming gifts.

1. Humility Born of Brokenness

A sure sign that we are making our way through is a keen, new awareness of our own sin and brokenness. The searing pain of a Wall reveals a secret that has always been true. We are in need.

Until this point, we could handle things pretty well on our own, thanks very much. But when suffering shows up on our doorstep, it breaks through our illusion of self-sufficiency.

Suddenly, we discover we are not immune from tragedy. No one is. Loss and failure are a part of every life. Even though no one in their right mind would ever choose it, a Wall offers us a gift we desperately need. It humbles us.

A Wall clicks off the autopilot mode of everyday life. It reveals our limits and our deep need for help beyond ourselves. As a result, we become less judgmental and more compassionate. We don't have all the answers we thought we did. Instead, there's more mystery.

A deeper awareness of our sin and brokenness helps us to see our common humanity with others, who also struggle with sin and brokenness. We stop worrying so much about the speck in our brother or sister's eye; we know the size of the plank in our own. And that humility born of brokenness is a gift.

2. Trust Deep Enough to Wait

Ever enjoyed waiting?

Me neither. My internal clock seems perpetually set to "hurry." But I've noticed in recent years that God doesn't have that setting. God's setting is far slower. Maybe that's why Scripture often refers to a different pace.

> *I wait for the LORD, my whole being waits,*
> *and in his word I put my hope.*
>
> —*Psalm 130:5*

One day, while I was on the eight-day retreat mentioned earlier, I joined a group that was silently "praying with clay." A big lump of gray clay was plopped in front of everyone, and we were supposed to let the clay become what it wanted to be (Really?). The point was to get us out of our own heads, but it mostly felt silly to me—until the next day.

That afternoon while praying outside under a shady tree, I suddenly saw in my mind's eye a multi-colored mass of clay undulating as if it was alive. Within seconds, two words emerged in large letters: Trust Me.

A moment later, it was gone. Nothing like this had ever happened to me. Other unique messages came my way as I spent increasing amounts of time alone with God. By the end of the retreat, I still didn't have concrete answers to all my questions, but God had revealed a new way of doing life and ministry that is diametrically opposed to my nature.

The unspoken mantra of my life had been "make it happen." I would get up in the morning, strap on my jet pack, and open the throttle. I might not know where I was going, but I was going to get there in a hurry.

I discovered that attitude can run you into a Wall, but it won't run you through one. Instead of "make it happen," God's invitation to me was "let it come." Go from tight-fisted control to open-handed surrender.

As we run through a Wall, we learn to trust God on a far deeper level—to let it come in God's way and God's timing. This method may not make any sense to us, and the timeframe will always be longer than we want, but the more we trust God to let it come, the easier it becomes to wait.

3. Freedom Found in Letting Go

Written into the DNA of American culture is the idea that we were all created by God with certain unalienable rights, including life, liberty, and the pursuit of happiness.

Since we are blessed to have life and liberty in this country, the question Americans routinely ask is "Am I happy?"

But that's not the right question. I love the way Peter Scazzero puts this: "The critical issue on the journey with God is not 'Am I happy?' but 'Am I free?'"[17]

The Apostle Paul was a church planter who wrote over half of the New Testament. As he was writing to the early Christians, he never once asked them if they were happy, but he was quite concerned about their freedom. To the Christians in Galatia, he wrote,

> *For freedom Christ has set us free. Stand firm, therefore, and do not submit again to a yoke of slavery.*
>
> *—Galatians 5:1 NRSVUE*

---

17.   Scazzero, Peter, *Emotionally Healthy Spirituality: It's Impossible to be Spiritually Mature, While Remaining Emotionally Immature*, Updated ed., Grand Rapids, MI: Zondervan, 2017.

Christ's work on our behalf was not only to set us free from the guilt of our sin but also the enslaving power of it. In Christ, we don't have to be bound by anything anymore: people's opinions, the lure of money, lust, pride, jealousy, laziness, a thirst for power, or addictions of any sort. We've been set free from those things, Paul says, so we must not submit to them again.

But we do. Lured by our culture and our selfish desires, we subtly begin to bow down again. The Wall is God's instrument to purge us of our various slaveries.

I've seen this purging power firsthand. In his later years, my dad used to watch a lot of sports on TV. He especially loved football. That all changed the day he was diagnosed with Stage Four Lung Cancer. It was a Wall like no other. He lived for three weeks after that and never once turned on the TV. He didn't want to spend his final days doing something that did not matter.

Walls have a way of revealing when our hearts have gotten attached to habits, attitudes, objects, or people in unhealthy ways.

Detachment is the key to inner freedom. The goal is not only to gain freedom *from* our excessive attachments but to experience a freedom *for* loving and serving God. This newfound freedom ushers us into a deeper, purer love for God and others.[18]

Of course, if you are like me, it's hard to know how attached you are to something until God takes it away. God got my attention on this topic during a recent message about giving away our stuff. The pastor pointed out how holding on to things is a form of hoarding that robs others of a blessing. He challenged us to give away 10 things that week. I went into my closet and gave away 144. Clearly, I was overdue. It's my goal this year to give away at least one thing a week, not to declutter my house but to free my soul.

Walls help us see unhealthy attachments for what they are—idols that cling to and control our hearts. They enslave us, but Jesus came to set the captives free!

Imagine what it would be like to say with the Psalmist,

> *And there is nothing on earth that I desire other than you.*
>
> —*Psalm 73:25 NRSVUE*

God uses a Wall not only to winnow out destructive attachments but to give us a gift. Through the long-suffering of a Wall, God imparts a transforming love into our soul.

---

18. Ibid.

In fact, when a Wall has done its full work, we will no longer feel a need for acclaim or success. Our desire is simply to do God's will. We will have learned Paul's "secret of being content in any and every situation".[19] There is a freedom found in letting go.

Made Perfect in Love

These gifts are transformative, in part because they cost so much. In fact, it may take more than one Wall to acquire them. I've been through three of them along the way (proof that I'm a slow learner). I'm guessing there will be more because I'm so far from being made perfect in love.

I'm still too concerned about what other people think of me and too controlled by fear. Despite God's loving-kindness, I'm still too easily irritated and too prone to overwork. Those things don't have the same hold on me they once did, but I'm not free from them yet.

To be clear, although I desire that deeper transformation, I'm not seeking a Wall to gain them. Nor am I wishing one on anyone else. But as we go through life, they come.

Here's the good news: the next time we have a crisis, and nothing makes sense anymore, when our prayers run out of words, and it feels like God has left planet, we don't have to ditch God or check out of church. We will know what is happening. We have Wall issues.

Here's what we will also know: the Wall is really a door.

It's not the end of our walk with God. It's the beginning of a deeper stage of our journey.

If we accept God's invitation to run through the Wall and take in enough soul food to sustain us, we can finish the race as someone transformed into love.

---

19. Philippians 4:12

CHAPTER FIVE

Puzzling with God

God has given each of you a gift from his great variety of spiritual gifts. Use them well to serve one another.

—1 Peter 4:10 NLT

God never loses sight of the treasure which He has placed in our earthen vessels.

—Charles Haddon Spurgeon

Ever heard of a dissectologist? I hadn't, but that didn't keep me from being one. It refers to someone who enjoys putting together jigsaw puzzles. The term comes from the original name for puzzles in the late 1700s—"dissected maps." In those days, wooden maps were carved into pieces to teach students geography. Over time, they morphed into the jigsaw puzzles we love today.[1]

Puzzles are like stories. They draw us in because we love to see how all the pieces fit together. Around the holidays, my dad used to dump out a large jigsaw puzzle on a cardboard table, and everyone would start sorting. First, we would find the edge pieces to make the border. Next, we sorted the middle pieces by color and pattern. The picture on the box helped us put them in the right area. Finally, we went through the painstaking process of finding the right fit for each piece in the grander scheme.

---

1.   Zimmerman, Devan, "What Do You Call a Person Who Loves Puzzles?" Blue Kazoo, August 10, 2023. https://bluekazoo.games/blogs/articles/what-do-you-call-a-person-who-loves-puzzles#:~:text=Dissectologist%20(noun)%3A%20A%20person,and%20for%20some%2C%20professional%20puzzlers.

Imagine a puzzle piece in your hand right now and think about God's box-top picture for this world. Each piece in this massive jigsaw represents a life, and every piece has its place in God's plan. Not one of them is optional.

Just ask Jack. At 86, Jack Harris was determined to finish the five-foot long, 5,000-piece puzzle he had been working on for over seven years. When he finally completed it, he stepped back to survey his masterpiece, only to find one piece missing! Mr. Harris searched the house from top to bottom, but alas, one of his family's two dogs may have swallowed it.

They even reached out to the manufacturer for a spare, but Mr. Harris took so long to finish the puzzle the company no longer makes it.

His daughter-in-law who gave him the puzzle said, "When we saw there was a piece missing from the middle, we just couldn't believe it…It's sad really because now it will never be completed."[2]

That's the power of one. For all the joy of 4,999 pieces in place, it is still one piece short. That's how important each person is in God's eyes. Without you, without your piece, God's beautiful design will not be complete.

To finish the picture, every follower of Christ must find his or her place in God's plan. Much like a jigsaw puzzle, it will take some time and effort to find the right fit. We might pick up our piece, turn it several different ways, and try a variety of spots. Of course, if it doesn't fit at first, we don't throw it away. We just keep working the puzzle. We know every piece is a perfect fit somewhere.

Each Part Matters

The Apostle Paul expressed this same conviction using the metaphor of a human body.

> *Just as a body, though one, has many parts, but all its many parts form one body, so it is with Christ. For we were all baptized by one Spirit so as to form one body—whether Jews or Gentiles, slave or free—and we were all given the one Spirit to drink.*
>
> *—1 Corinthians 12:12–13*

---

2. Allen, Vanessa, "Pensioner Spends Over Seven Years Doing 5,000 Piece Jigsaw Puzzle... Then Finds One Bit is Missing," Daily Mail Online, May 17, 2010. https://www.dailymail.co.uk/news/article-1278837/Jack-Harris-spends-7-years-doing-5-000-piece-jigsaw-finds-ONE-bit-missing.html.

In Christ, each of us is an indispensable part of his body, even though the individual parts are quite diverse. Without each one, the body would be incomplete and unable to function as designed.

Sadly, some think, "Well, I'm just one part. They'll never miss me."

Don't be fooled. Regardless of how small or seemingly insignificant, each part matters.

The way we hear is a perfect example. The three smallest bones in the human body are the middle ear ossicles, commonly known as the hammer, anvil, and stirrup. They work in total obscurity, unseen by an outside observer. Yet they are indispensable for us to hear. Without them, 99.9% of the sound waves that hit the eardrum would never make it to the inner ear. God has arranged these tiny parts to have a tremendous impact on our hearing.

It's the same in the body of Christ. There are no unimportant parts. Whether visible or invisible, up front or behind the scenes, each of us plays a vital role in God's unfolding drama of redemption.[3]

The Big Three

Of course, not everyone is aware of this life-changing truth. In their recent book, *3 Big Questions*, Kara Powell and Brad Griffin reveal landmark research from the Fuller Youth Institute involving 1,200 teenagers.

The study found that today's teenagers are the most anxious, adaptive, and diverse generation in history, which sometimes makes it hard for older generations to relate to them. While every teenager is a walking bundle of questions, three rise above the rest.

- Who am I?
- Where do I fit?
- What difference can I make?

Certainly, teenagers aren't the only ones who wrestle with these questions. Most adults roll through life searching for answers to the "Big Three" as well. The challenge for all of us is finding the right place to look.

---

3. "As the Human Body has No Insignificant Parts, so also the Body of Christ," Preaching Today, 2017. https://www.preachingtoday.com/illustrations/2017/july/6071717.html. (Adapted from Living Amazed by James Robinson, pp. 203–204).

Success Panic

A while back, a woman described a guy who had it all—a high-powered job, a big house, fancy cars, and memberships in all the right clubs. But he was the most miserable man she knew. When asked "How so?" she said, "Well, he hates his job, and he would like to quit, but he can't bear the thought of giving up the lavish lifestyle his job supports. He's stuck, and he hates it."

It's a familiar story. He suffers from a classic case of what some call "Success Panic." It is when we get everything we ever wanted, only to discover it's not what we truly need. It's a sinking, vacant feeling that threatens to suck our heart right out of our chest. In disbelief, we whisper, "I gave up my life for this?"

One of life's great ironies is that success in any area cannot deliver on the biggest promise it makes: it cannot bring fulfillment. At the height of his career, actor Jim Carrey said, "I wish everyone could get rich and famous and everything they ever dreamed of so they can see that's not the answer."

We are so much more than a possession accumulator or an achievement machine. We are spiritual beings created by God for a grander purpose in this world.

Take a look at these questions again.

- Who am I?
- Where do I fit?
- What difference can I make?

They are best answered by looking at God's big picture and finding our place within it.

Looking at the Box Top

A box top reveals the creator's intention for the pieces inside. God's big picture for our lives has four parts: God's desire, God's directive, God's destiny, and God's design. Let's start with desire.

God's Desire ➔ *A life-giving relationship with Christ*

A spiritual journey often begins with a question young children like to ask. "If God made everything, why did God make me?" A wise parent might respond, "God made you to love you." Scripture says, "God is love"[4], and love by its very nature seeks to be shared. That's why God's deepest desire in creating us is to enjoy a loving relationship. Through the prophet Jeremiah, God says,

> *"I have loved you with an everlasting love;*
> *I have drawn you with unfailing kindness."*

> —*Jeremiah 31:3*

If God really loves us this way, why do so many of us feel afraid and disconnected? Clearly, the problem is not on God's end. From the beginning, our selfishness and sin separated us from God's love. As every parent of a wayward child knows, God could not simply wink at willful disobedience as it deadened our lives, destroyed our relationships, and distanced us from God's presence. Sin has grave consequences. Yet at the same time, God wanted nothing more than to be in a loving relationship with us. Something had to be done.

Out of that desperate love, God created a bold, risky, never-been-tried strategy. God became one of us.[5] To bridge the great divide formed by sin and brokenness, the all-powerful Creator of the universe became a helpless child.

God must have thought, "Through my Son, I can take on human flesh. I will breathe their air, eat their food, and walk their streets. I will teach them my truth and show them my healing power. Then, they will understand how deeply I love them."

It was all part of a grander purpose. "Indeed, God did not send the Son into the world to condemn the world but in order that the world might be saved through him."[6]

God is on a mission, and contrary to what some may say, it is not to condemn people. God's mission is to save the whole world through the sacrificial love of his Son.[7]

By placing our faith in Jesus, he rescues us from the three greatest obstacles to a loving relationship with God—sin, evil, and death. Instead, we become a new creation by the Spirit—forgiven, redeemed, and full of life! We also discover a new purpose.

---

4.   1 John 4:8 NRSVUE

5.   John 3:16

6.   John 3:17 NRSVUE

7.   Ross, Roger, *Meet the Goodpeople: Wesley's Seven Ways to Share Faith*, Nashville: Abingdon Press, 2015, pp. 17–18.

Ever wonder why God did not take you to heaven the moment you accepted Christ's forgiving love and new life? Why didn't God rescue you from all the heartache and suffering of this world and transport you straight into eternal bliss?

It's all part of a bigger plan. When we come into a relationship with Jesus, we receive a new reason for living. Paul says, "For we are what he has made us, created in Christ Jesus for good works, which God prepared beforehand so that we may walk in them".[8]

In God's grander purpose, we are saved to serve. The reason we are still here is to do the good works God has prepared for us ahead of time. There are big tasks and small ones. Our job is to be on the lookout for the serving adventures God has already arranged.

Do you wonder what your adventure might be? You're not alone.

Leilani grew up as a missionary's kid. She came to know God's love as a child and wanted to share that love with others. She just wasn't sure how. In high school, she felt led to a career in nursing, because it could make a difference in someone's life every day.

She chose a college in the center of a large city and often interacted with unsheltered people before and after class. As she neared graduation, she met an unsheltered woman who had been on the streets since she was 16. When Leilani asked, "What's next for you? How can you continue to become well?"

The woman responded, "I need to help myself, because God always helps those who help themselves."

Leilani knew this false proverb would keep her new friend stuck right where she was, but even as a new nurse, she felt helpless to provide the whole person care this woman needed. Soon after that encounter, Leilani felt called to go to seminary. Her deep dive into Scripture and various ministry approaches was a time of great learning and growth. When she finished, she surprised those around her by immediately returning to nursing.

When asked why she would spend four to five years in seminary and not go into full-time ministry as a pastor, she said, "As I was praying and discerning during that time, I felt my calling was to do ministry outside the walls of the church. Now, I feel more ready to provide care not just physically, but spiritually."

8. Ephesians 2:10 NRSVUE

Leilani's heart desire is to serve others fully and faithfully in the name of Christ. Here's what she has discovered. Our deepest joy and greatest significance come when we serve. It is such an unlikely truth that many of us dismiss it without a thought. But the God who made us has no greater purpose for us than to see our lives transformed into the likeness of Christ. What might that look like? Jesus describes it in his personal mission, "For even the Son of Man did not come to be served, but to serve, and to give his life as a ransom for many".[9]

Strangely enough, the most powerful person who ever walked the planet came to serve. It was his core identity. He wasn't on earth to amass power, possessions, or prestige. Wealth or fame never made his list. His only concern was to do his Father's will and give his life for the sake of others. Jesus' epic journey of emptying himself to become a servant is captured by Paul in what most scholars consider an early Christian hymn.

Who, being in very nature God,
did not consider equality with God something to be used to his own advantage;
rather, he made himself nothing
by taking the very nature of a servant,
being made in human likeness.
And being found in appearance as a man,
he humbled himself
by becoming obedient to death—
even death on a cross!

Therefore God exalted him to the highest place
and gave him the name that is above every name,
that at the name of Jesus every knee should bow,
in heaven and on earth and under the earth,
and every tongue acknowledge that Jesus Christ is Lord,
to the glory of God the Father.

—Philippians 2:6–11

The immeasurable humility of Jesus to willingly leave the glories of heaven for the gore of the cross reveals a jaw-dropping, awe-inspiring love. For all who follow him, Jesus spells love s-e-r-v-e.

9. Mark 10:45

Before we can see the rest of the box top, we need to stop here and surrender our lives to Christ. God's deepest desire is to be in a life-giving relationship with us through his Son. If we choose to follow Jesus, we will take on the nature of servant, someone ever ready to follow the Master's direction.

God's Directive → *Make disciples of Jesus*

They were his last words. After three years of teaching and modeling how to live under God's reign, the resurrected Jesus gave this mission to his 11 disciples, minus Judas:

> *Therefore go and make disciples of all nations, baptizing them in the name of the Father and of the Son and of the Holy Spirit, and teaching them to obey everything I have commanded you.*
>
> —*Matthew 28:19–20*

Jesus packed so much in this great commission; let's narrow our focus to three life-changing points in the first eight words. The first is *Go.* As he and his disciples stood on a mountain in Galilee, the first words out of Jesus' mouth were not "Stay right here." His disciples may have preferred that. To share the message of Jesus would mean certain persecution and probable death. Jesus had already set the pattern. Staying there would have increased their comfort level and personal safety. But the mission was not to minister to one another in a holy huddle. As he had done numerous times before, Jesus was sending them out. He knew two-thirds of God is *go.*

Second, the purpose of going was clear: make disciples. Jesus had no interest in making fans or boosters or half-hearted followers. This was the man who said, "Whoever wants to be my disciple must deny themselves and take up their cross and follow me."[10] Half measures meant nothing to him. He was after their whole heart. Of course, allegiance at that level doesn't happen by accident. He commanded his ragtag band to be intentional, to make disciples. It's a process that incorporates new people, literally including people in the corpus, the body of Christ, through baptism and teaching them to obey all the things Jesus had commanded.

Third, Jesus' vision was breathtaking. He didn't tell his disciples to go only to their own people. They were to make disciples of *all nations*. Nations here means "people groups." To get the scope of this vision, imagine every

---

10. Matthew 16:24

group of people you know. In addition to groups most like yours, think of the groups you don't like, who say and do things you don't agree with, and who vote differently than you. Consider groups whose appearance, behavior, and style of dress are shunned or ignored by your group. Now, picture groups whose culture, ways of worship, and geographic location vary widely from yours. Finally, think of the groups you may consider your enemy.

Jesus wanted his followers to make disciples of these nations. It's a tall order by any measure. How on earth would that ever happen?

In his final resurrection appearance, Jesus gave his disciples the blueprint:

"But you will receive power when the Holy Spirit comes on you; and you will be my witnesses in Jerusalem, and in all Judea and Samaria, and to the ends of the earth."

—Acts 1:8

Standing in Jerusalem, Jesus charged his friends and faithful followers to be witnesses by the Spirit's power right where they were. They would then go to ever widening circles, including the Samaritans whom they despised, until the whole world was reached.

God's directive through God's Son is to make disciples of Jesus. As we do so, it leads to God's destiny for each of us.

God's Destiny → Be a full-time minister of Christ

Some of you may be thinking, "Oooh, I *knew* it! I knew if I got too close to this Jesus guy, I would have to slick back my hair and go to Africa as a missionary." Not necessarily. It may mean God is calling you to have lunch with your neighbor. Slicking back your hair is optional.

I understand the fear, though. If someone had told me in junior high that God wanted me to be a full-time minister, I would have gone in a corner and cried. At the ripe age of 13, I thought pastors were totally out of touch. They had to get special training, wear weird clothes, and take on a certain status in the community. I knew I could never fit into that straitjacket existence.

Besides, I had plans. From age eight, my big dream was to be a marine biologist. Jacques Cousteau was my hero (he's worth googling). Watching his TV specials about the ocean and its exotic life forms fascinated me.

Without a second thought, I dismissed any notion of full-time ministry. Of course, I never imagined that ministry might not be connected to being a pastor. Thinking back on it, I may not have been the only one.

In contrast, the early church had a completely different take on ministry—one Jesus modeled. When Jesus chose a common, hot-headed fisherman to be the rock on which he would build his church, he flipped everything upside down.

Apparently, a special training, a special garb, and a special status were not prerequisites for ministry in Jesus' kingdom. Of course, this unconventional approach was not lost on Peter. In a letter to everyday disciples, he declared,

> *But you are a chosen people, a royal priesthood, a holy nation, God's own people, in order that you may proclaim the excellence of him who called you out of darkness into his marvelous light.*
>
> *—1 Peter 2:9 NRSVUE*

"Wait a minute," someone might object. "Is he saying that all disciples of Jesus are priests?!" Yes. Yes, he is. "But I *can't* be a priest. I'm not qualified." Me neither. That's the funny thing about following Jesus. It doesn't matter. God doesn't call the qualified; God qualifies the called. Turns out, a real relationship with Jesus is enough to get started.

Before tossing that thought in the crazy bin, take another look at the last phrase Peter uses to describe his sisters and brothers in Christ: "God's own people." In the original Greek of the New Testament, that last word is a translation of *laos*. It is where we get the word "laity." But in Greek, it simply means *people*, as in a specific community with shared characteristics.

Peter is saying that regardless of our training or experience, we are all the people of God. In the early church, there was no two-tiered caste system of paid clergy and unpaid laypeople. The Bible knows nothing of professional Christians.

In fact, for at least the first one hundred years of Christianity, there were only the *laos*, the people of God. Some might wonder, "How on earth did the church survive?" It didn't. It thrived! The early Christian movement exploded through the Roman Empire, transforming a brutal pagan culture with an ingenious approach.

Disciples of Jesus practiced what we now call "the priesthood of all believers." They believed there were many ministries, and everyone in Christ is gifted in at least one of them. There was no artificial and unbiblical split between the professionals and the amateurs, the players and the spectators. Every follower of Christ was a minister of Christ.

Imagine what this scriptural truth could do if it were put into practice today. I've been to many churches that have an excellent pastor and some great staff members, but most of their time is tied up in running the church and taking care of church members. All the while, there are hundreds, thousands, or, in some cases, hundreds of thousands of people within easy driving distance who are spiritually adrift. How are these people ever going to know the love of God and become deeply devoted disciples of Jesus?

Do you think the best way to reach them is through a pastor? Sometimes, but for most people, that doesn't fly. Pastors are way too scary. Picture a pastor coming into your workplace or school. Someone unknowingly asks, "So, what company are you with?" The pastor says, "I work with God. We bring heaven on earth." Immediately, everyone would pull out their phone to see if a suspect was on the loose. After an awkward silence, someone would say, "Great... Lunch anyone?"

Relying solely on pastors might not be the best plan to reach people on a larger scale. Fortunately, God has a better idea. We know God's greatest desire is to be in a life-giving relationship with us through his Son. That means God loves every kind of people group. Do you suppose that would include nurses? Without a doubt. What might be the best way to reach a nurse? Perhaps through another nurse. I like the way Pastor Wayne Cordeiro talks about God's sneaky approach.

God takes full-time ministers and disguises them as nurses. It's true. God gives them compassion for their patients and gifts to be the best nurses they can be. Each day as they head into the hospital or clinic, they become God's vessel for sharing the love of Christ with other nurses – and patients too!

How might God choose to reach firefighters? The Lover of our soul is very crafty here. God takes full-time ministers and disguises them as fire fighters. They receive all the gifts and training they need to be both courageous and decisive in rapidly changing situations. God then assigns them to fire departments across the country.

What about mechanics? There is a plan for them too. God takes full-time ministers and disguises them as mechanics. God gives them gifts and a passion for fixing intricate machines, a high tolerance for grease, and then stations them in every town and city.[11]

God's Plan A to reach the world is to send full-time ministers everywhere. It is God's destiny for you and me regardless of our day job. Ministry is not a special domain reserved for pastors, evangelists, and church staff. It's for all of us. Every follower of Christ is a minister of Christ. God has chosen to make God's appeal to the world through us. There is no Plan B.

Just for kicks, give this a try. Write your name in the blank below.

_____, Minister of Jesus Christ

How does that feel? A little weird? That's OK. You'll get used to it. I had to when I became a disciple.

Here's the fun part. Next time someone asks what you do for a living, go ahead and share your day job, "I'm a salesperson, a student, a stay-at-home parent, an engineer, etc." While you're saying it, smile and whisper to yourself, "But that's just my disguise. Really, I'm a full-time minister." They would just die if they knew that.

Let's pause there and recap. God's greatest desire is to be in a life-giving relationship with us through his Son, Jesus. When we discover that kind of relationship, God's directive for our lives is to make disciples of Jesus. In fact, it is God's destiny that we be full-time ministers to reach the world God so desperately loves.

Fortunately, we are not left to do that on our own. God has something better in mind.

God's Design → *Use spiritual gifts for ministry*

God's design is to empower us through spiritual gifts to minister in supernatural ways. Discovering, deploying, and developing these gifts is a crucial mark of a deeply devoted disciple. Here's how we understand this fifth "G" called Giftedness.

A disciple sees his or her identity as a servant of Christ, discovers one's spiritual gifts, deploys them in ministry under God's direction, and develops them to their full potential.

---

11. Cordeiro, Wayne, *Doing Church as a Team: The Miracle of Teamwork and How it Transforms Churches,* Grand Rapids: Bethany House Publishers, 2022, p. 45.

A full discussion of spiritual gifts is beyond the scope of this book. For now, here's a quick look at how they operate. When we surrender our lives to Jesus Christ, the Holy Spirit gives us at least one spiritual gift, perhaps a cluster of two or three. Each gift is an attribute of Jesus. While on earth, Jesus displayed all the gifts: mercy, evangelism, serving, teaching, healing, leadership, discernment of spirits, and a variety of others.[12]

Since Jesus is no longer with us physically, the Spirit distributes one or more of the gifts to each follower of Christ. Paul described it this way:

Now there are varieties of gifts but the same Spirit, and there are varieties of services but the same Lord, and there are varieties of activities, but it is the same God who activates all of them in everyone. To each is given the manifestation of the Spirit for the common good.

—1 Corinthians 12:4–7 NRSVUE

These "manifestations of the Spirit" empower us to serve one another and build up the body of Christ. Since no one has all the gifts, we need each other. Every gift is essential for the whole to operate at full strength.

Our first step toward Spirit-empowered ministry is to discover our spiritual gifts. If we are not connected to a church that offers some teaching and guidance on this subject, a quick internet search will reveal many articles and books that can fill the gap. It is also fairly easy to find a spiritual gift inventory. Such inventories ask a host of questions to help us uncover our primary gift(s). While these tools are useful to a point, inventories by themselves can't reveal our spiritual gifts with certainty. It is possible to "game the system" so the results turn out the way we think they should.

The best way to discover our gifts is to dive into a particular ministry and see if God shows up. There are two defining characteristics of a fully operating spiritual gift: fruitful and fulfilled.

Fruitful means other people's lives are touched, changed, and encouraged through our service. Perhaps we see people come to Christ or grow in Christ. Those who experience our ministry feel a sense of life and hope. Entire groups move forward spiritually. Ministry objectives are met or exceeded. The body of Christ grows stronger and more loving.

At the same time, we notice our hearts are fully engaged, perhaps for the first time. We look forward to the opportunity to serve. It brings us life and

---

12. There is no widely agreed upon list of spiritual gifts. The New Testament has four key passages related to spiritual gifts: Romans 12:1–8, 1 Corinthians 12, Ephesians 4:4–16, and 1 Peter 4:9–11.

energy. Sometimes, it is straight up exhilarating. A voice inside us says, "I was born for this!" Jumping into a ministry that aligns with our gifts is deeply fulfilling.

However, one out of two of these characteristics is not enough. I've known people who were fruitful but felt exhausted, not exhilarated. They simply didn't enjoy that form of serving. It wore them down and stole their joy. In such cases, serving in that area may be a competency, but it is not a gift.

In contrast, some people are absolutely enamored with exercising a particular gift. As they serve, they are happier than a pig in clover, but no one else is. In fact, the more they serve in that area, the less those around them live in faith, hope, and love. Over time, the Spirit ebbs away and the ministry declines. A lack of fruitfulness simply means that form of service is a personal preference rather than a spiritual gift.

In these situations, we may need to help people find their true giftedness. We know a spiritual gift is at work when a person is both fruitful and fulfilled.

Of course, this experience rarely happens the first time we dive into the serving pool. Typically, we need some time to try out a serving opportunity to get the feel of it. If, after numerous attempts, we realize it is not fruitful *and* fulfilling, we swim to another spot and give that a try. This process may be repeated several times before we find our sweet spot of serving.

Discovering our gifts takes commitment, to be sure. But knowing the pure joy of being used by God for something greater than us far outweighs the effort.

Once in that sweet spot, God *deploys* us as a full-time minister. That's when our gifts are put to work. Jesus knew that adults learn best in on-the-job training. Instead of having his disciples sit in class day after day for years before getting any real-world experience, Jesus flipped the script. He gave them some basic orientation and deployed his disciples as soon as possible. They came back with successes, failures, and a boatload of questions. That's when they were ready to be *developed*.

In this development phase, we claim the spiritual gifts God has given us, load up our questions, and begin to truly learn. We go to conferences and read books. We consult mentors, coaches, and people in similar ministries in an all-out effort to improve and grow.

Pastor A. R. Bernard said, "Life is God's gift to us. What we do with it is our gift to God." Developing our spiritual gifts is a crucial part of the gift we give back to God.

Remember the "3 Big Questions"?

- Who am I?
- Where do I fit?
- What difference can I make?

Many of us are driven by FOMO (Fear of Missing Out). Afraid we won't discover who we really are or where we fit, we feverishly try everything paraded in front of us. Others of us throw up our hands in resignation, believing we have missed our chance. Either way, what keeps us up at night is a question on auto repeat: "Does my life make any difference?"

Maria Stenvinkel, a corporate consultant from Sweden, asked 65 people from around the world, "What's your greatest fear in life?" Not surprisingly, people mentioned the fear of "dying alone" or "losing my job." But of these 65 people, at least 14 (more than one in every five) expressed a different fear—living life without purpose or meaning.

In their own words:

My biggest fear is never taking a risk in an effort to find my true calling.

—Anthony, New York City

My greatest fear is to go through life living small but not realizing it until it's too late.

—Rebekka, Stuttgart, Germany

My greatest fear would be missing out on my purpose here on earth. … I know I have a purpose that I am not yet serving.

—Danielle, Sacramento

To go through life without leaving a positive mark.

—Luciana, Sintra, Portugal

My greatest fear is regretting all that I didn't do, as I lay in my hospital bed as an elderly man.

—Ralph, North Brunswick[13]

---

13. Stenvinkel, Maria, "A Surprising 'Greatest Fear in Life," Preaching Today, December 19, 2016. https://www.preachingtoday.com/illustrations/2020/september/surprising-greatest-fear-in-life.html.

Does the fear of living a life without purpose haunt you?

If so, consider once more these truths. God's greatest desire is to love you and be in a life-giving relationship with you through his Son, Jesus. Jesus' life on earth, his death that defeated sin and evil, and his resurrection to new life prove your infinite worth in God's eyes. Beyond a shadow of a doubt, you matter to God.

In this life-giving relationship, you have a purpose—to love God and make deeply devoted disciples of Jesus. This directive is so important, God called and destined you to be a full-time minister in your everyday life. Beyond that, God has given you spiritual gifts to ensure you have a vital role in God's redemptive drama.

Your singular life is more valuable in God's eyes than you could possibly know. Take a moment and imagine your puzzle piece again. Roll it around in the fingers of your mind. Your piece reveals two crucial facts about you.

First, it says you have a shape. A wise pastor in my life would often say, "You will never know who you are until you know Jesus Christ." Apart from Christ, we will never know our unique shape. The edges will be undefined, and the picture blurred. Left to ourselves, we will fashion our own shape and try to force our piece into places it doesn't fit.

Second, your piece tells you how much you need others to discover your God-given purpose. No matter how valuable it may be individually, your unique shape finds its true purpose only when connected to others in God's larger picture.

In fact, seeing how we fit in God's box top vision of the world stirs a generous spirit in us to turn that big picture into reality.

Life Multiplied

It is more blessed to give than to receive.

—*Jesus, Acts 20:35 NRSVUE*

"I sure didn't expect that."

Jenny had just received a call inviting her to a new church starting in her city. When she explained who had called, her husband grilled her, "You didn't give them any money, did you?"

"Of course not," she said, but in her heart, she felt a glimmer of hope. She and her husband had moved to the area two years before and hardly knew a soul. She felt lonely and thought perhaps this would be a way to meet new people.

Tim, however, had no such interest. After some bad church experiences and a thorough investigation of religion in college, he became a professed atheist. What irritated him most about churches was their constant appeals for money.

Although not fully aware of it, Tim carried three prevailing attitudes about money and giving.

First, he quietly fretted, "What if I don't have enough?" Although he and Jenny both had high paying jobs, they always seemed to be running short. In his mind, they simply couldn't afford to give anything, even if they had the desire—which they didn't.

Second, Tim adamantly believed, "My money is mine." He'd earned it, and he intended to keep it for whatever his heart desired—a list that just kept growing.

Third, Tim was convinced, "They don't need my help." Wary of the many stories of scams in religious and charitable organizations, he couldn't justify the risk. Besides, those groups seemed to do just fine without him.

When it came to money, Tim was nobody's fool. He couldn't be more different from my friend, Jim. One day, a while back, Jim texted to say he was coming to town and needed a place to stay. He had been spending too much money lately and wondered if he could stay at our house on Friday night. After checking with my wife, I told him, "Sure."

Due to his commitments that night, Jim didn't arrive until after 11. We talked for a while, but we were both tired, so we called it a night. Early the next morning, I left for a prayer meeting at church. By the time I got home, he was gone…but not completely.

When I walked by the room where Jim had stayed, I noticed a note on the bed. It was for our son, Zach. The note thanked him for giving up his room, encouraged him in his studies and sports pursuits, and gave him a $10 bill. We were like, "Really? Who does that?" Zach was totally surprised. He had slept at a friend's house that night and didn't even know Jim was there.

Later that day, Jim realized he forgot the cord to his phone. His weekend was too packed to pick it up, so he stopped by the office on Monday just before noon. He said, "Hey Rog, let me take you for a quick lunch." I already had plans, but he insisted.

As we ate, Jim asked what was happening in my life and really wanted to know. He offered some very helpful advice on a knotty issue and promised to send me further info the next day (which he did).

As we finished our meal, he pulled out a gift card to pay for it. When the bill came, he planned to give a 20% tip but that would have left a few dollars on the card. Instead, he gave the whole amount to our server, at least a 40% tip.

When I commented on his big-heartedness, he laughed, "Someone gave me that. It's not really mine. It came from their hand to my hand and now to our server's hand. It's all the Lord's anyway."

Naturally Attractive

Do you know anybody like this? Every time Jim turned around, he found a way to be generous. Here's the weird thing about it. He wasn't even trying. It just oozed out of him. How does that happen?

I don't know about you, but I love being around people like that. There's a winsomeness about generosity. It is naturally attractive. Not so when the polarity is reversed.

I've lost count of the number of families that have blown up over who's going to get what when their last remaining relative dies. Bitter fights over "what I deserve" and "getting what's coming to me" tear some families apart.

Just as there's an attractiveness to generosity, there's a repulsiveness to greed. We have a natural aversion to greedy people. Technically speaking, we feel "icky" around them. Deep down, we know they are just in it for themselves. It's all about how much they can get. Wise King Solomon, likely the richest man the world has ever known, put it this way:

All day long the wicked covet, but the righteous give and do not hold back.

—Proverbs 21:26 NRSVUE

To covet means to reach out and grab for more. It's how the wicked operate. In effect, Solomon offers us a question: "Which kind of person do you want to be? Someone who is always reaching and grabbing for more or someone who gives and does not hold back?" A perk of following Christ is discovering the joy of giving.

On our journey with Jesus through the last five chapters, we have seen how Glory, Grace, Group, Growth, and Giftedness mark a deeply devoted disciple of Christ. Now we will center on our sixth and final G: Generosity.

Here's how to recognize it: *a disciple humbly recognizes all of life belongs to God and cheerfully gives his or her time and resources to bring Christ's healing, justice, and hope to those in need.*

Generosity is a Lifestyle

Jesus describes a generous life within a broader context of how his followers are to live in this world.

"Do not judge, and you will not be judged. Do not condemn, and you will not be condemned. Forgive, and you will be forgiven. Give, and it will be given to you. A good measure, pressed down, shaken together and running over, will be poured into your lap. For with the measure you use, it will be measured to you."

—Luke 6:37–38

For years, I heard this Scripture and never really understood that last part. In Jesus' day, "a good employer who pays the harvester with grain fills the measuring jar, shakes it to make more room, presses it down to make still more room, and then fills it to overflowing before pouring it into the worker's shirt, which the worker is holding out like a sack."[1]

What a beautiful picture of the generosity of God! Pressed down, shaken together, running over, until it pours into our lap. God's love, God's forgiveness, God's blessings are so abundant they fill our lives to overflowing!

But the real question is, "Can it be poured through our lives to others?" Can those of us who are fearful, tight-fisted, and selfish become trusting, openhanded, and self-giving? If my friend Jim is any indication, the answer is yes. But how? One way is by encountering God's character.

A Window to God

Amazingly, God uses material means to reveal who God is and who we were created to be. We gain a window into God's character when we face the three common attitudes about money and giving mentioned earlier. The first hits close to home.

- What if I don't have enough?

At some point, everyone asks this question. Ironically, concerns about having "enough" plague people of all income levels from unsheltered persons to the mega rich. "Enough" is a relative term. It is not based on one's means but on one's mindset.

Constant concern about adequate resources is a sure sign of a scarcity mindset. It's human nature to think, "There is only so much pie, so I must keep track of who gets what piece."

However, some of us are gripped by the specter of scarcity. Generally, there are two camps. The first includes people who grew up in a home that never had enough or were later struck by an experience that left them in great need.

The second form of scarcity pops up around misguided priorities and a missing plan. If we don't tell our money where it should go, it will go wherever it wants, which usually means out the door. Living life without sound

---

1. Green, Joel B., *The CEB Study Bible*, Nashville, TN: Common English Bible, 2018, Luke 6:38 notes, p. 120 NT.

priorities and a spending plan regularly leads to panicked shortfalls, no matter how high our income.

Contrast this fear of falling short to the Apostle Paul, who wrote to the early Christians in Philippi,

> *I have learned the secret of being content in any and every situation,*
> *whether well fed or hungry, whether living in plenty or in want.*
>
> *—Philippians 4:12*

In a consumer culture driven by daily ads designed to create discontent, how much would core-level contentment be worth? What did Paul learn that our age doesn't know? Just this: in any and every situation, God is a *provider.* That's how Paul could encourage the believers who worried about not having enough.

> *And this same God who takes care of me will supply all your needs from his*
> *glorious riches, which have been given to us in Christ Jesus.*
>
> *—Philippians 4:19 NLT*

Paul lived in utter confidence because time and again, God had shown up when all his resources had run out.

Have you ever had to trust God to supply your need?

Years ago, my parents helped to put me through college. But when I sensed a call to ministry, it meant four more years of study, and I knew I was on my own. I applied for as much financial aid as possible, worked all through seminary, and took out more loans. By the time I reached the second semester of my final year, I was completely tapped out.

I remember the day I received a bill from the school that had to be paid to graduate, and I didn't have the money. Perhaps you know that sinking feeling. I had already asked some friends for personal loans, but asking other young pastors for a loan was like trying to get a cat to bark. Even if you got it, it wouldn't amount to much. (Side note, I learned it is always best to borrow from pessimists. They don't expect it back).

With loans up to my eyeballs and my parents responsible for three more kids to put through college, I didn't know where to turn. I was desperate.

In a last-ditch effort, I went to the financial aid officer of the seminary and pleaded my case. I told him the whole story and how much I would like to graduate. Finally, I said, "I don't know what else to do. Is there any way you can help me?"

Without a hint of hope, he replied, "Let me take a look." He shuffled through some papers and in a deliberate tone said, "It appears there is some money in a denominational student fund. I will grant you $1,000."

For a moment, I sat in stunned silence. "You will?" I said. It was too good to be true. That was exactly what I needed to pay my bill and graduate! I thanked him profusely and nearly floated out of the room. Of course, that amount may not seem like much now, but to a guy who had less than nothing, it felt like a million dollars.

Here's what that experience taught me as a young adult. God can be trusted. God will provide in ways that we cannot see or imagine right now.

Deep down, I knew I didn't head off to seminary on my own; I was led to do that. But that incident was a huge confirmation. Apparently, I wasn't the only one who wanted me to graduate. God cared about that, too.

What the Holy Spirit impressed upon me that day was a profound truth God's people have long known: *where God guides, God provides.*

Since then, I've seen God's provision play out countless times in my life and the lives of others. Our God is a provider who loves to supply the needs of God's children. Our job is simply to ask, do our part, and trust God for the rest.

The second attitude is about ownership.

- My money is mine.

Every parent of a toddler has heard one word more times than they can count: "mine." In fact, it's a healthy part of our development. As a newborn, we have no concept of self. We see ourselves as an extension of our primary caregiver. Around 18 months, we begin to develop a separate sense of identity. Soon after, we boldly announce to the world our first possessive pronoun. "That book is *mine.*" "That toy is *mine.*" "That dog is *mine.*"

At this age, declaring possessions is not a sign of being spoiled. These special belongings have become a part of a child's emerging identity. Having them around helps children understand who they are and increases their sense of security.[2]

---

2. Milburn, Jessica, "'Mine, Mine, Mine!!'" Responsive Parenting, August 21, 2022. https://responsiveparentingblog.com/2022/08/21/mine-mine-mine/.

Ever wonder if this security need is real? Try taking away a toddler's treasure. A child's absolute certainty about what is "mine" makes this age both comical and crazy-making. T. Berry Brazelton captures it perfectly in the "Toddler's Creed:"

If I want it, it's mine. If I give it to you and change my mind later, it's mine.

If I can take it away from you, it's mine.

If I had it a little while ago, it's mine.

If it's mine, it will never belong to anyone else, no matter what.

If we are building something together, all the pieces are mine.

If it looks like it's mine, it's mine.

However, what's funny in a two-year-old loses its charm later in life. Before we become a follower of Christ, we may sound a lot like a toddler. "That house is mine." "That car is mine." "That money is mine."

When we become a Christ-follower, a big shift occurs. We move from "mine" to "Yours, Lord." We stop thinking of ourselves as the owner of all our stuff. Instead, we surrender everything to God as the rightful owner. King David described the shift this way,

> *The earth is the LORD's, and everything in it,*
> *the world, and all who live in it;*

> *—Psalm 24:1*

Once we make God the owner, we take on a new role. We become the manager of everything we have—every breath, every thought, every day, every thing.

On a practical level, it looks like this: my house, my car, my furniture, my clothes, my income, my bank account, my retirement savings, my books, even my golf clubs (gulp) are not mine. They are God's.

Here's how I know they are not mine. When I die, I'm not taking any of them with me. Over the years, I've done a lot of funerals, and I have yet to see a U-Haul behind a hearse.

In a letter to his young friend, Timothy, Paul wrote,

> *For we brought nothing into the world,*
> *and we can take nothing out of it.*

> *—1 Timothy 6:7*

Getting a grip on how life begins and ends helps us hold things lightly in the middle. When God says, "Thank you for managing that property, that possession, that investment, that thing; I have need of it now," we can let it go freely. It's not ours. We don't own it. It belongs to God. We've just been managing it for a little while.

When "mine" becomes "Yours, Lord," we can live in open-handed freedom. In this new mindset, we begin to appreciate things for what they are—gifts placed in our hands for a brief time.

God's character as a provider and an owner completely inverts our common attitudes about giving. The third attitude uncovers an even deeper dimension of God's heart.

- They don't need my help.

To be fair, some of us don't contribute our time or resources because we don't know where to start. Just following the daily news cycle brings compassion-fatigue. The sheer volume of need numbs us from feeling any responsibility.

Others of us are so worried about being scammed or so caught up in our own lives that we don't make any room for the needs of others. An often-unspoken thought is, "I have to make it on my own. Why can't they figure out life for themselves?"

Case in point, one Christmas eve, worship attenders were invited to write a Christmas card to unsheltered men and women after each of our services. One person wrote, "Quit drinking and get a job!" Fortunately, that one was never sent. There's a coldness in that attitude that disconnects us from others and their true needs, but it also disconnects us from God and our true needs. Something deep down is not working right.

Recently, my wife discovered our kitchen sink was clogged. We took some pipes apart, used a snake, and called a family member for advice, but nothing worked. Finally, we called a plumber. He identified the clog and removed it, but it took a while. Ten years' worth of gunk had accumulated down there. Thankfully, as soon as he removed it, the water flowed freely through the pipes.

Ever had a clog in your life? In some cases, an inner clog can build up for years until one day, nothing flows through us anymore. How does that clog get removed?

Jesus had a simple answer: "Give, and it will be given to you."[3] To most people, this clog buster makes no sense. That's no way to amass a fortune. To build wealth, we must hold onto and stockpile what we have. Yet, Jesus literally commands the opposite behavior. It is all part of his invitation to a different way of life.

People who offer undeserved love to others discover that such love comes back to them in unexpected ways. Those who forgive find that they are forgiven, and those who give receive more in return. This turnabout is so counter-intuitive, it surprises us with joy every time.

It is God's irrational math: *when we give things away, we receive more.* That's because God gives to us what God knows will flow through us. But to experience this serendipitous supply, we must go first. It's an act of faith.

Of course, we don't always receive material resources in response to material giving. God's provision comes in various ways, including spiritual courage and insight, emotional and physical healing, relational reconciliation and belonging, as well as a newfound purpose and peace, to name a few. These are not the kind of gifts one finds at a store. Frankly, they are far more valuable and enduring. Best of all, such gifts are tailored to provide for our true needs not our passing wants.

Ironically, giving is not just about helping others in need. We also have a need—to be saved from a clogged life. There's so much more God can do *in* us when we allow things to flow *through* us.

A second clog buster is more about being than behavior. Arguably, the most famous verse in the Bible is John 3:16. Some call it the gospel in miniature.

> *For God so loved the world that he gave his one and only Son, that whoever believes in him shall not perish but have eternal life.*
>
> *—John 3:16*

This single verse reveals volumes about the heart of God. Let's break it down.

"For God so loved the world…" Out of immeasurable love, a specific action flowed: God gave. A sure sign of love is giving something of great value to your beloved.

What did God give? A gift of incalculable worth: God's one and only Son.

---

3. Luke 6:38

For what purpose? To rescue the ones God loves from perishing and give them a with-God life that never ends.

And who are the ones God loves? You and me.

At the absolute core, God is a giver. Jesus, God's Son, was the perfect reflection of the Father in human form. He revealed God's heart when he gave his very life on the cross for you and me to save us from sin, evil, and death, so we could be forgiven, redeemed, and filled with life.

By putting our faith in Jesus and inviting his Spirit to reside in our hearts, the giving nature of God gets reproduced in us. Our hearts begin to reflect God's heart, and we become like our Creator—a giver.

Just ask Tim. At his wife's request, he begrudgingly went with her to that new church in town. To his dismay, it scrambled all his preconceived notions. The people were open and friendly. The music was modern, and the message actually made sense. He didn't want to like it, but he couldn't help himself.

Out of curiosity, he came back the next Sunday. He thought, "Maybe they just had an off week. They'll show their true colors soon enough." With jaded skepticism, he kept waiting week after week for the mask to slip. Along the way, his own mask started slipping.

Tim began to see that the people were authentic, the teaching was relevant to his daily life, and (gasp) they didn't ask him for a dime! Everything he thought he knew about God and church fell away in light of the love and truth found in that fledging family of faith.

One Sunday, Tim walked into a service with a hat that read, "Under New Management." In an astonishing turnaround, he decided to resign as the CEO of his life and turn everything over to Jesus.

Here's how that played out. The guy who was so resistant to giving pushed aside his high-paying engineering consulting job to be the church's first administrative assistant *as a volunteer*. Tim said, "I felt like God wasn't interested in me earning as much money as possible. My wife had a good job with good insurance, so that covered our bills. I was trying to lean into how God was leading me, and I knew that God would provide for us."

Eventually, Tim got a master's degree from a local seminary and went on to pastor churches in Michigan and Indiana. Now, he serves as a fundraiser at the seminary he attended. Yes, a *fundraiser*. Only God.

His kids joke that their dad has consistently worked his way down the ladder of success. Yet, Tim and his wife have always been able to give generously to whatever God has placed in front of them.

No one could have foreseen this level of heart change. Tim's relationship with Jesus turned his life upside down and transformed him into a giver—and he couldn't be happier about it.

Imagine what it would be like to allow the heart of God to be reproduced in our heart. Could giving change our lives, too?

Scientists in Switzerland wondered the same thing. Through MRI brain scans, they tracked activity in regions of the brain connected to socializing, decision-making, and happiness as people gave to others.

Remarkably, they found even small acts of generosity sparked brain activity that made people happier. In fact, just promising to be generous triggered happiness regions in the brain. Study participants also self-reported increases in happiness as they gave to others. Conversely, those who used resources only on themselves reported lower levels of happiness.[4]

A friend of mine sums it up this way: "Money can make you happy—when you give it away."[5]

In a "me first" culture, this is big news! Generosity is literally built into our brain chemistry. That helps explain what many of us have witnessed: the happiest people in life are givers.

In fact, the most noticeable characteristic about Tim these days is how happy he is. His co-workers tease him, "What is the matter with you, Tim? Why are you always smiling? What are you trying to hide?"

To our surprise, God doesn't want giving *from* us. God wants giving *for* us so we can experience God's supernatural supply, know true joy, and reflect God's character. We were made to be generous.

But we will never discover this fundamental truth until we take a specific action. We can't think or talk our way into it. At some point, we must simply give. Only then can we come to know God as a provider, an owner, and a giver, who loves to unleash torrents of compassion through clogless people.

A Force for Change

Generosity is a powerful force for change, and God knows we need the help. Other countries have their own struggles, but in America, the leading causes of death are self-inflicted—side effects of tobacco, obesity, alcohol, sexu-

---

4. Mozes, Alan, "Givers Really are Happier than Takers," Medical Xpress, August 15, 2017. https://medicalxpress.com/news/2017-08-givers-happier-takers.html.

5. Rev. Joel Labertew, Teaching Session on Stewardship, 3-2-25.

ally transmitted disease, drugs, and violence. Alarmingly, U.S. suicide rates have increased 40% between 2000 and 2020[6], while rising 62% for people ages 10–24.[7] The long-term effects of racism and poverty shorten lifespans and undercut human flourishing for large segments of the population.

On many levels, our culture is in a hope freefall. Although political policies matter, the law alone cannot fix such things. Something must happen in a person's heart.

Sadly, that's a tall order for millions of people who are skeptical of all things related to faith and church. In their view, church is anything but a change agent. It serves rather as a standard bearer of the status quo. Too often, that's painfully true.

But that's not Jesus' vision for his followers. He reveals his dream for our lives in the model prayer he taught his first disciples.

> *Our Father in heaven,*
> *hallowed be your name,*
> *your kingdom come,*
> *your will be done,*
> *on earth as it is in heaven.*
> *Give us today our daily bread.*
> *And forgive us our debts,*
> *as we also have forgiven our debtors.*
> *And lead us not into temptation,*
> *but deliver us from the evil one.*
>
> *—Matthew 6:9–13*

For countless Christians, this is a bedrock passage. It might be the only Scripture many people know by heart. Some of us pray it every day. Others pray it during weekly worship services. It's a cornerstone of Christian faith.

Notice the first request in this prayer. It asks for God's kingdom to come on earth as it is in heaven. This single line is a game changer. Many think that church is about trying to get people into heaven, but that's not what Jesus taught his disciples to pray. It is not about getting people into heaven but get-

---

6.   Noy, Shakked, "What Accounts for the Rise in Suicide Rates in the US?" NBER, July 6, 2023. https://www.nber.org/bh/20232/what-accounts-rise-suicide-rates-us.

7.   Curtin, Sally C. and Matthew F. Garnett, "Suicide and Homicide Death Rates Among Youth and Young Adults Aged 10–24: United States, 2001–2021," Centers for Disease Control and Prevention, June 15, 2023. https://www.cdc.gov/nchs/products/databriefs/db471.htm.

ting heaven into people! His prayer asks for God's rule, God's will, to be done on earth the way it is in heaven.

When we understand Jesus' vision of heaven on earth, we start to see church differently. Loads of us both inside and outside of church see it as a fortress. Although it may not be said out loud, there's a sense that church is where like-minded followers gather behind walls to protect us from the corruption of the outside world. Ironically, many church buildings have the imposing look of a fort. Of course, there are Scriptures that seemingly support this view.

> *The name of the Lord is a strong tower.*
>
> *—Proverbs 18:10 NRSVUE*

> *I will say of the Lord, "He is my refuge and my fortress,*
> *my God, in whom I trust."*
>
> *—Psalm 91:2*

We sing hymns like "A Mighty Fortress is our God," and that's all true. But each of these is talking about the nature of *God*, not the church. Jesus' vision for his followers is to be part of a kingdom on the move.

He said, in effect, "I'm inviting you to be part of a new way of living. Let me give you a glimpse. The kingdom of God is like a sprinkle of yeast that makes the whole loaf rise. It's a dash of salt that can preserve a full slab of meat. It's a tiny seed that grows into a great tree where birds of the air will come to nest."

In Jesus' kingdom, the tender will of God contagiously spreads to the ends of the earth. He invites his followers not to hunker down behind a fortress but to infiltrate this world as a *force*.

In fact, this was Jesus' favorite sermon. He spoke about the kingdom more than any other topic—more than love, prayer, or faith. In his teaching and ministry, Jesus mentioned the church three times. He spoke about the kingdom 92 times. Small wonder the first request in the prayer he taught his disciples is, "Your kingdom come, here and now!"

As we pray this prayer day after day, week after week, it's meant to shape both our hearts and our churches. How is the visible body of Christ in the world going to show up—as a fortress or a force?

When it acts as fortress, the church has little effect on the world around it. But when it serves as a force of God's love bringing heaven to earth, it unleashes a generous compassion on both a personal and societal level.

Generosity's Personal Touch

In a recent small group gathering, each of us shared places where we had seen the glory of God in our lives. Several people chimed in with personal stories: a special family trip, a new job, a dad's spiritual conversation with his son, and other such things. Nothing too unusual until Bob shared his "glory sighting."

Bob is retired and happily involved in the ministries of his church, including a shift at the county food pantry each Thursday. The night before, he always prays that God will send him someone he can really serve.

Earlier that month, a couple showed up who had just come to town. They were originally from the area, but the husband had been in prison for 13 years. Unfortunately, his father refused to let them live with him. As a result, they had been living on the streets and in the woods for the last few days. That morning, the woman had been attacked by a pit bull requiring a trip to the Emergency Room to get stitched up.

As the couple told their story, they couldn't hold back their tears. Bob prayed with them and felt led to offer some emergency funds in addition to food from the pantry and some food vouchers to a grocery store. He also discovered they only had the clothes on their back, so he gave both of them a set of clothes and a backpack. In very practical ways, Bob set them up well for the next few days.

Oddly, as they were leaving, Bob felt prompted to do something he had never done before. He gave them his phone number and said, "If you have other needs I can help with, give me a call."

At this point, every pair of eyes in our group widened. Bob explained, "I just felt God telling me that I needed to help these people. It was pretty obvious that they came to me for a reason, and I was supposed to help them."

They called the next day. The man, whom I'll call Jon, asked if they could stay with Bob for a while to clean up and take care of his wife's wound. Without hesitation, Bob picked them up, brought them to his house, and proceeded to help them "get their feet back on the ground."

After three failed interviews, Jon landed a job with a construction company, which was the job he really wanted. Bob is also working with them to get a car, so Jon can get back and forth to work. Beyond their physical needs, Bob is spending a lot of time in spiritual conversations.

Jon is well acquainted with religion. He was actively involved in a church growing up. That is the problem. His father, who considered himself a faithful Christian, was also highly abusive. The pain and hypocrisy from his home life left Jon bitter toward the church but, amazingly, not toward God. He re-engaged with his faith in prison, spending time in Bible studies and playing in the worship band for the prison chapel.

Bob and Jon have had many conversations about God, and Jon is very open. He just can't figure out Bob. As they talk, Jon will sometimes break down when describing what he's been through and say, "Why are you so nice to me? No one has ever been nice to me like this. I've never had anybody that I could trust or count on."

Sadly, Jon doesn't know what love looks like. Both his parents were in-volved with drugs. His dad still is. Bob described his relationship with Jon this way: "It's been a journey, and we are growing together. I'm getting close to Jon because he just needs a dad so badly. It's kind of an easy thing for me because I've had kids, and I know what that is like. Ironically, he is exactly the same age as my son."

Of course, not everyone could or should do this kind of thing, but Bob was clear about his reason why. "I have everything. I have a house. I live by myself. It felt like God was saying, 'If you can't help them, who is going to do this? It's you. You have to do this.' To me, I didn't really feel like I had a choice. I prayed about it, they showed up, and if I don't do this, I'm turning my back on God."

When Bob had finished his story, you could have heard a pin drop. God's glory had entered the room, and we felt its weight. We all felt convicted by the sacrificial love Bob showed to a struggling couple who landed on his doorstep.

James, the brother of Jesus, describes this kind of street-level spirituality:

What good is it, dear brothers and sisters, if you say you have faith but don't show it by your actions? Can that kind of faith save anyone? Suppose you see a brother or sister who has no food or clothing, and you say, "Good-bye and have a good day; stay warm and eat well"—but then you don't give that person any food or clothing. What good does that do?

So you see, faith by itself isn't enough. Unless it produces good deeds, it is dead and useless.

—James 2:14–17 NLT

In fact, Bob's ongoing generosity is what the Bible would call true justice.

Most people think of justice as a way to fairly punish wrongdoing. When the guilty are penalized, we say, "Justice has been served." However, the biblical concept of justice is much larger and more relational.

The word for justice in Hebrew is *mishpat*. It occurs over two hundred times in the Hebrew Old Testament. At a basic level, it means to treat people equitably. In other words, everyone should be given the same punishment for the same crime, regardless of origin, race, creed, social status, or other identity factors.[8]

But *mishpat* is more than that. It is also about giving people their rights and caring for the most vulnerable in our midst.

> *This is what the LORD Almighty said: 'Administer true justice; show mercy and compassion to one another. Do not oppress the widow or the fatherless, the foreigner or the poor.*
>
> *—Zechariah 7:9–10*

In ancient agrarian societies, these four groups—widows, orphans, immigrants, and the poor—were completely powerless and teetered on the edge of survival. Today, this list would surely include unsheltered people, the severely addicted, some single parents, and the elderly.[9]

From a biblical viewpoint, the measure of a just society is based on how its most vulnerable are treated. If the needs of these groups are not met, it is not a failure of charity. It's a failure of justice (*mishpat*).

Thankfully, in every age, the vulnerable among us have had at least one strong Advocate.

> *For the LORD your God…defends the cause of the fatherless and the widow, and loves the foreigner residing among you, giving them food and clothing.*
>
> *—Deuteronomy 10:17–18*

The connection is hard to miss. If God loves and defends the poor and the powerless in our society, it's our calling too. That's how we "do justice."[10]

---

8.   Keller, Timothy, *Generous Justice: How God's Grace Makes Us Just*, New York: Penguin Books, 2016, p. 3.

9.   Ibid., p. 4

10.   Ibid., p. 5

This is where Bob got it so right. By a prompting from the Holy Spirit, he didn't simply offer this couple basic freebies that could get them through a day or a week. He opened his life and his home to help alleviate their gaping needs and restore them to self-sufficiency. Bob is extending a generous justice—the kind the Lord commanded the people of Israel to offer.

> *If anyone is poor among your fellow Israelites in any of the towns of the land the LORD your God is giving you, do not be hardhearted or tightfisted toward them. Rather, be openhanded and freely lend them whatever they need.*
>
> *—Deuteronomy 15:7–8*

When we take up the care and cause of the vulnerable in our midst, we are doing justice. The work is costly, to be sure, but such giving is a special form of generosity that grabs the attention of the world around us and brings God glory.

Of course, Bob is not the only one doing this kind of thing. In his classic book, *Bowling Alone*, Harvard professor Robert Putnam reports that "religious Americans are more likely to give money to a homeless person, return excess change to a shop clerk, donate blood, help a sick neighbor with shopping or housework, spend time with someone who is depressed, offer a seat to a stranger, or help someone find a job."

But it doesn't stop there. "Regular church attenders give almost 4 times as much money to charity as their secular neighbors and twice as many of them do volunteer work among the poor, the infirm, or the elderly."[11]

When the grace of God takes hold of a human heart, it has a way of transforming an otherwise tightfisted person into a new creation whose generosity brings healing, justice, and hope. As miraculous as that is on a personal level, wait until you see what can happen on a larger scale.

Sowing Social Fabric

When members of Grace Church in Cape Coral, Florida began prayerfully walking and driving through their community and the Ft. Myers area several years ago, they saw things in some places that broke God's heart: homelessness, drug houses, addiction, and a pervasive loss of hope.

---

11. Yancey, Philip, *Vanishing Grace: Bringing Good News to a Deeply Divided World*, Grand Rapids, MI: Zondervan, 2018, p. 164.

While discerning what this meant, a guest speaker came to their church. In her talk about God's deep love for a community, Deb Hirsch said, "The heartbeat of the city is where the pain is."

Her words brought God's vision into focus. Grace's ministry would land in three big buckets: the special needs community, people facing addiction, and those caught in poverty. Over time, the vision led them to acquire a site downtown where they could work directly with unsheltered people and serve those who desire to be in recovery.

To better serve this mostly non-churched population, Grace Church began partnering with a ministry called Better Together to organize to meet one of their community's deepest needs. Better Together's mission is to keep families together and children out of foster care by providing kids with a temporary, loving home, while helping their parents build a better life. Job loss is often a root cause of many serious issues, including child neglect. To address that challenge, Better Together partners with churches around the country to put on community job fairs.[12]

These half-day job fairs bring a massive infusion of hope to the community—but not without a lot of effort. Grace's planning process alone takes six months. All three campuses of Grace Church contribute to this project. They supply the facility, as well as 100 volunteers, many of whom take off work to be part of the miracle of life change.

On the day of the fair, hundreds of job seekers arrive at the church. As they enter the parking lot, people are greeted and offered a job coach. The coach helps them build a resume or brush up an old one, discern the kind of work for which they are gifted, and talk through potential interview questions. Coaches often pray with applicants before they go into a room with employers.

Prior to any interviews, applicants at Grace's job fairs have numerous services available on site to encourage their success.

- A thrift store to provide clothes for interviews
- A cosmetology school that offers free haircuts and beard trimming
- Representatives from the DMV to obtain a driver's license or update one

---

12. Better Together | Keeping Families Together, Accessed September 26, 2024. https://bettertogetherus.org/.

- Lawyers to have a record expunged or help with other legal issues

- Mental health professionals to provide free counseling and support

- Health insurance professionals to help register for government health care

- Child trafficking and domestic abuse awareness groups to help with any past or current issues

- Representatives from several sober living houses who offer residential support to overcome addiction

- Leaders from Grace Church who share practical and spiritual resources from parenting classes to small group Bible studies to recovery ministry in a worshipping community

Of course, there is also an amazing group of employers from 25–30 local companies and non-profits. Since Grace specifically hosts Second Chance job fairs, each organization is friendly to people who have prison sentences or other background issues. They encompass a diverse set of enterprises such as landscaping, construction, cleaning companies, school districts, restaurants, and a large health system.

One might wonder, does all this effort make any difference? At a recent job fair, 398 job seekers were served and 58 people were hired on the spot! Many others lined up promising second interviews. Wes Olds, senior pastor of Grace Church, calculated that the unemployment rate in the county dropped 1.5% that day.

Imagine the ripple effect of joy through the community. It's what happens when the church unleashes the kingdom force of generosity on a societal level. This immense display of collaborative compassion keeps families together, heals deep wounds, and takes up the care and cause of the most vulnerable among us. It's the fulfillment of Scripture.

Speak up for those who cannot speak for themselves; ensure justice for those being crushed.

Yes, speak up for the poor and helpless, and see that they get justice.

—Proverb 31:8–9 NLT

When asked what he loves most about these twice-a-year Second Chance job fairs, Larry Frank, pastor of the Ft. Myers Central Grace site where the fairs take place, replied,

> The hope that comes with it. This is an underserved community. We are two blocks away from downtown where homeless people sleep and drug deals happen in the parking lot. I love the smiles on people's faces who feel treated with dignity and respect. They know there is a church and ministry that cares about them. They are not alone. The job fair helps them know they can do this, even if they didn't get hired on the spot that day.

Perhaps the most gripping testimony comes from another leader of Grace Church, whose life was forever changed. Victoria was homeless, addicted to drugs and alcohol, and incarcerated at 23. She spent three years in prison. Released on parole, she made her way to her parents' home in Southwest Florida on a Saturday.

On Tuesday morning, she saw a newscast about the Better Together Second Chance job fair at Grace Church. Her Mom said, "You have to go. You have to try."

Amazingly, she walked out of the fair that day with two job offers. As she tells it, "Being out of prison only four days, I would not have believed you if you had told me I would have been sober, going to church, working full-time, and really good at my job. This job fair gave me a second chance."[13]

Surprisingly, it gave her even more. Victoria met her future husband that day. They are now married and have a child together. She has recently been promoted to a management position in her workplace and serves on the Central Campus Operational team at Grace Church. Her story is just one of many unfolding miracles.

Imagine with me for a moment. What if everyday disciples humbly placed their lives and their resources in the hands of a God who loves them? And what if they saw themselves individually and collectively as a kingdom force bringing heaven to earth? How many broken lives would be restored? How many families would be brought back together? How many communities and schools would be safer and stronger? These scenarios don't belong in the realm of wishful thinking. They are happening right now in places like Cape Coral and hundreds of other cities across the nation.

---

13. Video, Better Together | Keeping Families Together, Accessed September 25, 2024. https://bettertogetherus.org/

Healing, justice, and hope came into many people's lives, including Victoria's, because a fantastic team of deeply devoted disciples demonstrated extravagant generosity. The same thing could happen in your city and mine if we take this sign of a disciple to heart. Unleashing this kind of compassion turns the tide of hurt and injustice. It is part of what makes the church the hope of the world.

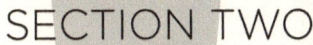

SECTION TWO

Disciples Who
Make Disciples

Soul Sync

We're probably not going to slip one day and fall into Christian maturity.

—*Martha Grace Reese*

One day, it hit me. I had no rhythm.

I'm not referring to dance floor moves (although I don't have those either). It had more to do with an inner sense of timing. I was working hard, trying my best, but things just weren't coming together. Below the emails, activities, and never-ending meetings, something was out of sync. I felt a longing for more.

Don't get me wrong; I had a very good life. It was full of great people, engaging challenges, and significant work. But I couldn't shake this feeling that I was missing something.

Too often I was lurching from one project to the next. Deadlines, which I generally consider helpful, began to stack on top of each other. During certain stretches, it felt like I was constantly preparing for, leading, or recovering from some ministry event. Living like that was shrinking my soul.

Ironically, I came to a point where the more I served Christ, the less connected I felt to him. That's not what Jesus had in mind for his followers. It's not the kind of life I wanted either.

In a chance conversation with a co-worker, he recommended a book by Ruth Haley Barton called *Sacred Rhythms*. In it, Barton describes this longing beautifully.

> *Your desire for more of God than you have right now, your longing for love, your need for deeper levels of spiritual transformation than you have*

> *experienced so far is the truest thing about you. You might think that*
> *your woundedness or your sinfulness is the truest thing about you or that*
> *your giftedness or your personality type or your job title or your identity as*
> *husband or wife, mother or father somehow defines you. But in reality, it*
> *is your desire for God and your capacity to reach for more of God than you*
> *have right now that is the deepest essence of who you are.*[1]

Maybe you feel a longing for more too. Although it's the truest thing about us, our desire for God can be squelched by the way we do life. It may not be blatant sin holding us back. It may simply be an issue of reordering our life.

Finding our rhythm has been a quest of disciples of Jesus for a long time. In the sixth century, St. Benedict was the first to create a "rule of life." It was a simple way to order the everyday lives of monks living in community to grow deeply devoted disciples.

Spiritual transformation cannot be boiled down to a formula. There will always be a God dimension that remains a mystery. However, Benedict, those in his order, and countless millions of Christ-followers since have discovered the enormous value of a structure that helps us say yes to God.

In fact, the word "rule" comes from the Greek for "trellis." In a vineyard, a trellis is used to lift grapevines off the ground. As the vines grow upward, they produce more fruit. When we embrace a rule of life, it helps us abide in the Vine and live more fruitful lives.

Spiritual writer, Peter Scazzero, defines a rule of life this way: "an intentional, conscious plan to keep God at the center of our lives."[2] That's no small task these days. Our level of distraction far exceeds what life was like just 15 years ago, let alone 15 centuries ago. If followers of Christ needed a rule to help them become deeply devoted disciples in a medieval, agrarian society, imagine how valuable it could be for us now.

As 21st century disciples, we desire to love God, launch community, and unleash compassion. Signs that we are living that kind of life can be found in the six G's: Glory, Grace, Group, Growth, Giftedness, and Generosity. Each of these G's contains a myriad of spiritual practices to tune out distractions and keep God at the center of our lives. However, it is our job to discern which practices work best and in what combination.

---

1. Barton, Ruth Haley, *Sacred Rhythms: Arranging Our Lives for Spiritual Transformation*, Downers Grove, IL: InterVarsity Press, 2006, p. 24.

2. Scazzero, Peter, *Emotionally Healthy Spirituality: It's Impossible to be Spiritually Mature, While Remaining Emotionally Immature*, Updated ed., Grand Rapids, MI: Zondervan, 2017, p. 190.

God is more than willing to show up in our lives if we are willing to make room. The issue is more about how deeply we desire it. Have we had enough of living out of sync? In the Gospels, one man's desire ran so deep, it took everyone by surprise.

Our Deepest Desire

The encounter occurred near the end of Jesus' earthly ministry. As he traveled north from southern Judea to Jerusalem, he passed through Jericho.

By this time, Jesus' miracles and teaching had caused such a stir, crowds lined the streets to catch a glimpse of him. As his entourage passed the northern gate of the city, a blind man was sitting by the roadside, begging. Hearing that Jesus was nearby, Bartimaeus shouted out: "Jesus, Son of David, have mercy on me!"[3]

His loud pleas annoyed the crowd because they couldn't hear what Jesus was saying. People yelled at him to pipe down, but Bartimaeus shouted all the louder, "Son of David, have mercy on me!"[4]

Amazingly, Jesus stopped and called him out of the crowd. When face to face, Jesus looked at him and asked,

"What do you want me to do for you?"

—*Mark 10:51 NLT*

Seems strange, doesn't it? His blindness had to be obvious, but Jesus doesn't assume what Bartimaeus wants. He may have a life-threatening illness. His daughter may be on the verge of death with a fever. Maybe his marriage is crumbling, and a supernatural change of heart is needed.

Imagine Jesus is looking at you right now, and he asks, *"What do you want me to do for you?"*

What would you say?

Maybe something like: *"Help me. Heal me. Love me. Show me the way. Save my marriage, rescue my child, restore my family. Change this situation or give me the strength to get through it."*

What do you want Jesus to do for you, really? It is likely something only he could do.

---

3.   Mark 10:47 NLT

4.   Mark 10:46–52 NLT

When Jesus asked that of Bartimaeus, there was no hesitation. "My Rabbi, I want to see."

His answer released his healing. Jesus said,

> *"Go, for your faith has healed you." Instantly the man could see,*
> *and he followed Jesus down the road.*

> —*Mark 10:52 NLT*

Bartimaeus' faith became the channel for God's healing power to restore his sight. The moment that happened, he left his old life to follow Jesus in a new way of life.

What do you desire more than anything else in your life right now? Take a moment and write that down. It may be a new beginning point in your spiritual life.

When I realized I was out of sync, it revealed my deeper desire. I had plenty of church. What I longed for was more of God. I needed a new rhythm.

Top Priority

Once I named that desire, God revealed something that reoriented my entire life. For nearly 30 years, I had subconsciously put church on the top of my priority list. My first unspoken question every morning was, "What do I have to do for church today?" I would figure that out and make everything else fit around it.

Imagine my surprise when God showed me that I had put the wrong thing on top. As important as church was, it wasn't God. It was the work I did to serve God. When I looked at it that way, my first question every morning didn't sound nearly as spiritual: "What do I have to do for work today?" Should that really be my top priority?

I wanted to put God first, not my work. In fact, I wanted to demote work to somewhere below my family. Thankfully, the Spirit dropped in my mind a much better question: *what do I need to do to live in the presence of God today?* Once I figured that out, I could make everything else fit around it.

This was a seismic shift for me. I had never consistently looked at life this way, and I knew to make this change, I would need to seriously reorient how I lived each day. To be honest, I didn't know if I could do it, but I really didn't have another choice. I was sick of living the other way.

What is the first question you ask yourself every day?

- What do I have to do for work?
- What do I have to do for school?
- What do I have to do for my family?
- What do I have to do for my health?
- What do I have to do to please my dad or my spouse?
- What do I have to do to save this relationship?
- What do I have to do to entertain myself?

Here's how you can tell. As you wake up, what are the thoughts that spontaneously come to mind? "Oh, I need to drop off the kids, send that email, call that person, go to that meeting, buy that thing, etc." Those are "answers" your mind is generating to a question that is often unspoken. If, for instance, all those answers have to do with your work or how you can please your spouse, you know the deeper question.

What if you changed the question to, *what do I need to do to live in the presence of God today?*

Like all good questions, this one flipped the script for me. I began to see life from a completely different angle. It's not about getting stuff done. It's about being in the Presence. I love the way spiritual writer Dallas Willard describes this.

> *The main thing God gets out of your life is not the achievements you accomplish. It's the person you become.*
>
> —*Dallas Willard*

Daily reorienting my mind toward living in the Presence was precisely what I needed get back in sync. But it didn't happen in a week or two. I had to dig deep into basic truths about how we grow spiritually and create some sacred rhythms to support this new way of being.

Sacred Rhythms

Early one January, I went to a nearby retreat center, turned off everything with a switch, and spent a couple of days alone with God to listen, think, and pray. In the quiet, God revealed three truths about transformation that helped me get started.

- I can be transformed, but I can't transform myself.

It is a paradox of the Christian journey. There are things I can do to be inwardly transformed, but I can't do the transforming. That's the Holy Spirit's work.

It's like growing plants. We can provide all the right conditions, the best soil and fertilizer, as well as the right amount of water and sunlight, but we can't make the plant grow. Only God can give the growth.[5]

Spiritually speaking, the right conditions for growth exist when we practice spiritual disciplines that open us to the inner work the Spirit does by grace. That's the second truth.

- Practicing spiritual disciplines opens my life to be present to the Presence.

Again, Dallas Willard's wisdom is helpful here:

Grace is not opposed to effort; it's opposed to earning.

We can't earn God's love, but we can place ourselves in a position to receive it. John Wesley often quoted a Scripture passage that reveals this dual nature of spiritual transformation:

…continue to work out your salvation with fear and trembling, for it is God who works in you to will and to act in order to fulfill his good purpose.

—Philippians 2:12–13

In the soil of a soul well-tended, our Master Gardener grows the sweetest fruit. The third truth revealed a way to do that tending.

- Grace grows in a life rhythm of rest, solitude, community, and ministry.

Each element is crucial to work out our salvation.

- Rest requires us to stop all our doing, so we can contemplate and delight in God's many gifts. It includes activities that bring renewal.

---

5. 1 Corinthians 3:7 NRSVUE

- Solitude consists of time alone with God. It opens the eyes of our heart to the indwelling presence of the Holy Spirit.

- Community is doing life together in worship, conversation, learning, and prayer. Here we experience the intimacy of the Holy Spirit through our relationships with others.

- Ministry involves serving others in Christ's name. As full-time ministers in disguise, we serve others in our everyday work.

Below is a general list of spiritual practices that could fall under each of the four categories.

Rest	Solitude
Sabbath	Prayer
Family Time/Date night	Bible reading & reflection
Game night	Journaling
Time with friends	Examen
Exercise	Nature walks alone
Hobbies	Personal retreats
Holiday breaks/Vacation	Spiritual reading
Community	**Ministry**
Meet new people in my area	Serve others in my home,
Host neighborhood gatherings	my workplace,
Launch a new small group	my church family,
Engage in an existing small group	my community and the world
Connect with others in local com-	Personally share my faith
munity groups & events	Take up the care and cause of the vulnerable

Identifying our spiritual practices and making them a regular rhythm of our life is what opens our hearts and lives to spiritual transformation.

Creating a rule of life is not a "set it and forget it" exercise. I have been making and remaking my rule for years. Once we put something together, we try it for a while to see if it helps keep God at the center. If not, we discern what needs to change, adjust, and try again. It usually takes a few months to live into a new rule. Pro Tip: don't try this by yourself. Band together with two or three others and agree to lovingly hold one another accountable.

After discerning what would work for me in the four areas above, I've found it helpful to design my rule of life in concentric circles with each ring representing a different measure of time: daily, weekly, monthly, quarterly, and annually. I've also connected each of them to their primary G, although many of these practices involve more than one G. Here are a few examples from my rule to show what it looks like to use this format:

Daily

Glory

- Meditative Prayer: Spend 20–30 minutes silently worshiping in the chapel of my heart

Grace

- Examen: Review the day in the evening or the next morning to discern times of consolation (moving toward God) or desolation (moving away from God)

Growth

- REAP Bible Reflection & Journaling: Connecting what God reveals in Scripture with journaling my thoughts, feelings, and prayers

Giftedness

- Serve Others Through Coaching, Teaching & Writing: Use my spiritual gifts to come alongside pastors, leaders and their teams to help them thrive

Weekly

Glory

- Corporate Worship: Meet weekly with a large group of Christ-followers for worship, teaching, and connection

- Sabbath: Set aside a 24-hour period each week to stop, contemplate, and delight. Includes time with family and friends, playing games and unplugging from social media

Grace

- Faith-Sharing: Personally share my faith with at least one person weekly

Group

- Men's Group: Meet with a small group of men to confess our sins, encourage one another and pray for each other to be healed

Growth

- Temple (of the Holy Spirit) Maintenance: Physically exercise to stretch and strengthen my body at least four times a week

Generosity

- Justice & Hope: Serve those in need through a dinner church for unsheltered and underserved persons

Monthly

Generosity

- Tithe & Offerings: Give at least 10% of my income to the work of God through the church and make special offerings to advance the mission of Jesus

Quarterly

Glory

- Extended Sabbath/Vacation: Take three to four day breaks each quarter

Annually

Glory

- Vacation: Take at least one vacation that lasts a minimum of two weeks

These are some of the disciplines that help me stay in rhythm. Your set of practices will be different from mine, but we each need specific ways to help us become more like Jesus. Like him, we need a life rhythm of rest, solitude, community, and ministry.

You may be wondering, what difference does this make? In my experience, quite a lot. I don't live out all my practices perfectly. I certainly find myself reverting to old habits at times. But by God's grace, some noticeable transformation is happening.

A while back, I was feeling a great sense of anxiety and foreboding. To make matters worse, it felt like God was indifferent to my circumstances. Maybe you know what it is like to say, "Hey God, I'm freaking out here, and it feels like you don't even care!"

Fortunately, I had already set a time to talk with my spiritual director. When I explained my near paralyzing fear, he encouraged me to use my imagination and have a conversation with Jesus.

He said, "Tell Jesus, 'Here I am. I'm anxious but you're disinterested.' How would Jesus respond?"

I was quiet for a few moments. Finally, I replied, "He would say, 'It is I. Do not be afraid.'"

My spiritual director said, "How would you respond to that?"

"I'd probably say, 'That's good, Lord. I'm glad you're here. But why should I not be afraid? For what good reason?'"

"And what would Jesus' response be?" he asked.

What came to me was, "Because I am here."

By this time, I was getting the knack of it, so I continued, "I'm glad you are here and that you are with me. I really need that, but I don't know what to do about all these things I'm facing."

I sensed Jesus say, "I know what you're facing."

"That's great, Lord," I responded. "Then what should I do about them?!"

"Trust me," he said (an all-too-common theme in my walk with Jesus).

At this point, my spiritual director couldn't hold back any longer. "Roger, this is a revelation of God's will for you now. The real issue is not the content of the fears but rather, 'Will I trust in you, Lord, now?'"

Frankly, that was the last thing I wanted to do. A large part of me wanted to control it, but in the end, I let go and surrendered my circumstances.

Later that day, without me lifting a finger, two of my biggest sources of anxiety were resolved. A few days later, the other one was, too.

120

Of course, I was thrilled with the outcome, but what left a greater impression on me was the profound power of trust. Since then, there have been other circumstances I surrendered into Jesus' hands that didn't turn out as well. That's when I learned the true meaning of my spiritual director's wise words; "The real issue is not the…fears, but rather, 'Will I trust in you, Lord, now?'"

Earlier in my life, the answer was a flat no. But my soul is more in sync now. To be honest, that makes the crucial difference.

If you have a longing for more of God and want to see greater fruitfulness in your life, creating a rule of life, a trellis, to help you stay more connected to the Vine may be your best hope.

In fact, it may start with a simple question each morning: *what do I need to do to live in the presence of God today?*

Jump in the River

Our world is hungry for genuinely changed people.

—Richard Foster

The last thing they wanted to do was go to church.

Mike and Jamee had been married for less than a year when friends invited them to the first service of a new church in town. Let's just say, they were not thrilled. They had both left church years before and had no desire to be part of a new startup. But instead of making a fuss and straining their friendships, they hatched a plan. They would agree to try the church on the first Sunday and then tell their friends it was simply not for them. It was a small price to pay. The service would only last an hour.

It never occurred to them that the presence of God might show up that day. As they got in the car after the service, Jamee asked Mike what he thought. He said, "You're not going to believe this, but I think we should go back." Jamee replied, "You're not going to believe this either, but so do I."

And go back they did, week after week. Participating in that church slowly changed their personal lives, their marriage, and their family.

Fast forward to today. Mike is now an ordained pastor serving in a regional leadership position that influences hundreds of churches. Of course, a lot happened in between. More on that later.

When I first met Chantel, the one word that could describe her life was frenetic. She and her husband had three young kids. They also had full-time jobs, a house, a boat, various friends, and more things to do than any ten people could manage on a given day. Chantel had some experience with church growing up, but the whole relationship-with-Jesus thing never clicked for her. She saw church as a place for rules and rituals, most of which she didn't understand.

One Sunday, as she sat in a pew, she heard the pastor talk about God's grace and immediately had an emotional response. It caught her off guard. Somewhere inside, she had a deep desire for something more, a longing for God, but didn't know where to start.

Still searching, she began to work for a Christian non-profit that sends humanitarian aid to people in need. As she met all kinds of staff and volunteers, she kept wondering, "Why are these people so happy?" Slowly, it dawned on her. They were happy because they were serving others. Serving changed her too.

Now, Chantel serves as the director of that Christian non-profit. Each year, her organization sends $7 million of medical, educational, and disaster related supplies to places across the US and 15 countries around the globe. Their mission is to send tangible resources to make an intangible difference in people's lives. Obviously, a few things occurred in between. I'll get to that in a moment.

As a sales rep, Shane was rapidly climbing the corporate ladder. What no one knew was how empty he felt on the inside. In his search for answers, he anonymously tried a church and was surprised to find the messages spoke to him personally. Some weeks brought encouragement, others conviction, but always application. He appreciated that part the most. Eventually, he came out of the shadows and sought a deeper connection.

Today, Shane continues to knock it out of the park in his corporate job, but he also serves as bi-vocational pastor. In a few short years, the church he serves has been transformed from an older, declining congregation to a growing community of faith, filled with young families and hope.

The in-between part was quite a journey. Let's get to some of that.

Up to this point, we have placed considerable emphasis on what a disciple looks like. A deeply devoted disciple loves God personally each day, launches community with the people in his or her sphere, and unleashes compassion to a world in great need. We have detailed the marks of this Life in 3D with six G's and shown how each G includes an inward experience of God coupled with an outward expression of faith.

Making a Disciple

The question that begs to be answered is "how do you make one of those disciples?" Of course, there is a divine component to this process that is well beyond our pay grade. But like all spiritual transformation, there is also a human element. If we take specific actions, the odds of making a disciple greatly increase.

The first of those actions is to change a common mindset about church. Former Chaplain of the United States Senate, Richard Halverson, summarized the history of Christianity this way:

> *In the beginning the church was a fellowship of men and women centering on the living Christ. Then the church moved to Greece where it became a philosophy. Then it moved to Rome where it became an institution. Next, it moved to Europe, where it became a culture. And, finally, it moved to America where it became an enterprise.*[6]

As an enterprise, most US churches are not designed for conveying the gospel. They are designed for consuming it. The pandemic exposed that weakness. As we went through an extended period of restricted gatherings, racial reckoning, and political division, the church was severely limited in the menu it could offer its customers. The response was immediate. People who had been serving in their church for years up and quit. Long-time members evaporated from the scene. Many churches experienced significant financial shortfalls. Others closed altogether.

When churches were able to safely reopen, less than half of their regular attendees returned. That percentage gradually increased, but many church leaders discovered that around a third of their pre-pandemic worship attenders chose not to come back. They simply had to draw a new line and start from there.

Contrast this with the persecution of Christians for a 30-year period in China from 1949 through 1979. During that time, religious groups of all kinds were persecuted. Religious buildings and churches were confiscated by the government. Foreign missionaries were deported. Throughout the Cultural Revolution of 1966–1976, all religious activities were banned, and reli-

---

6.   Richard Halverson Quote, AZ Quotes, Accessed December 18, 2024. https://www.azquotes.com/quote/534191.

gious leaders were targeted for persecution. Christians were forced to practice their faith in secret.[7]

When the religious ban finally ended, many thought Christianity had died. How could it survive with no church buildings, professional clergy, or foreign missionaries for so many years? It didn't. It thrived the way the early church did. The number of protestant Christians had grown from 700,000 in 1949 to 10 million in 1979—a 1,300% increase![8] Catholicism also grew dramatically.

In fact, the Chinese church continues to grow. As of 2010, conservative estimates put the number of protestant Christians at 58 million along with 12 million Catholic Christians.[9]

What made the difference? A clear focus on making deeply devoted disciples. Pastor Larry Walkemeyer explains this kind of disciple-making approach with a powerful metaphor. He describes two kinds of churches: a lake church and a river church.[10]

Lake Churches are like bodies of water that don't move. Their goal is to grow the lake bigger by adding more and more attractions for people to consume—programs, activities, services, dinners, fall festivals, sports leagues, etc. As a rule, lake churches are very focused on what happens at their building. They want everyone to stay in one place so the lake can grow. A river church takes a different approach.

River Churches invite people to jump in a current that helps them find God and live as disciples of Jesus. This transforming process results in deeply devoted disciples who carry Jesus' love to others downstream.

Oddly enough, some river churches don't have a building. They meet in "underground" groups in people's homes, much like the Chinese church did

---

7. Nadeem, Reem, "Government Policy toward Religion in the People's Republic of China – A Brief History," Pew Research Center, August 30, 2023. https://www.pewresearch.org/religion/2023/08/30/government-policy-toward-religion-in-the-peoples-republic-of-china-a-brief-history/#:~:text=1966%2D1976:%20Mao%20Zedong's%20Cultural%20Revolution&text=During%20the%20Cultural%20Revolution%2C%20religion,were%20abandoned%2C%20closed%20or%20confiscated.&text=Chinese%20people%20who%20wanted%20to%20maintain%20their%20faith%20practiced%20in%20secret.

8. Pittman, Joann, "Bamboo Resilience: Christianity's Explosive Growth in China," Desiring God, July 29, 2024. https://www.desiringgod.org/articles/bamboo-resilience.

9. "Global Christianity – A Report on the Size and Distribution of the World's Christian Population," Pew Research Center, December 19, 2011. http://www.pewforum.org/2011/12/19/global-christianity-exec/.

10. Ferguson, Dave and Warren Bird, *Hero Maker: Five Essential Practices for Leaders to Multiply Leaders*, Grand Rapids: Zondervan, 2018, p. 100.

and still does in many places. Others have multiple locations to reach people in various regions. Still others send people and resources to start new congregations in unreached population centers. The building is a sidebar. River churches are always flowing somewhere to make more disciples.[11]

Here are some general characteristics of each kind of church:

<u>**Lake Church**</u>	<u>**River Church**</u>
Attractional (Come to us)	Missional (Go to them)
Members come to be served	Members go to serve others
Makes institutional members	Makes incarnational disciples
Grow the church	Advance Jesus' kingdom
Program-driven	Spirit-led

Simply put, lake churches are about adding to their pool and keeping each person close. River churches are about multiplying and sending disciples into an ever-flowing river that brings life to everything it touches.

In the first half of my life, all I ever knew was a lake church. I was raised in that kind of church, studied them in seminary, and was mesmerized by the "great lakes" as a young pastor. But one day, something shifted in me. On a trip to the Holy Land, we went to the Dead Sea. It was an eerie experience. Before us was this huge body of water, but no plants or trees were around it, and no fish or marine life could live in it. Our guide told us the Dead Sea has six times the salinization of ocean water. It is dead because water flows into it, but nothing ever flows out of it.

I immediately knew I didn't want to be a Dead Sea Christian. Nor did I want to serve that kind of church. Jesus said, "Whoever believes in me…rivers of living water will flow from within them."[12] He did not call his followers to be a resevoir, but a river. That's the vision I deeply desired, although I had no idea what that might mean.

By God's grace, I have seen many people turn their lives over to Christ and become disciples through their church. In preparation for this book, I asked several people if they would share what helped them become deeply devoted disciples. Listening to the way the Holy Spirit worked in their lives was both thrilling and revealing. Along the way, a pattern of disciple-making

11.   Ibid.

12.   John 7:38

emerged that I had not seen before. I have used the acrostic RIVER to explain it. Here's how the pattern unfolds.

Relay

Life in the Spirit is an ever-flowing river. We receive from the Holy Spirit, and we pass on what we have been given to others. There are two gifts we regularly receive that are meant to be shared: spiritual teaching and the power of God.

In his earthly ministry, Jesus engaged in both proclamation and demonstration of the gospel. He taught the word of God with authority, and he demonstrated the power of God through healing, serving, and expelling evil. Paul did the same. In his letter to the believers in Corinth, he said,

My message and my preaching were not with wise and persuasive words, but with a demonstration of the Spirit's power, so that your faith might not rest on human wisdom, but on God's power.

—1 Corinthians 2:4–5

When we relay to people what God has revealed to us through prayer, a Scripture, a song, another person, or a life event, we are passing on what God initially entrusted to us. We are also making room for more revelation to follow. Sometimes the teaching itself applies so directly to someone's deepest need, it becomes the demonstration of God's power. At other times, we show God's power by some act of healing, service, or overcoming evil with good.

In a recent conversation with a young man of no particular faith, he confided he was having terrible nightmares. Night after night, he dreamed someone was chasing after him with a knife and other such scenarios that deeply disturbed him. When I asked how I could pray for him, he was dumbfounded. "No one has ever asked me that before," he said. After a pause, he still didn't know how to answer. I replied, "No worries. I'll pray as the Spirit leads." From that day on, I began praying for God to heal him of his nightmares.

When I saw him about a month later, I asked how his dreams had been. He brightened up immediately. "You know, they've been pretty good lately. Just random stuff but nothing scary." He paused for a moment and said, "Hey…wait a minute. Have you been doing something there?" I smiled and

127

said, "Maybe a little praying." That may have been the first time in his life he recognized the power of God at work in him.

We demonstrate God's power in large group settings when we open a time for people to come forward for prayer, anoint people with oil for healing, or commission people for a specific form of service.

Relaying spiritual teaching *and* the power of God turns on a light that awakens people to their desire for more of God. That's exactly what happened to Mike, Chantel, and Shane at the beginning of this chapter. Once spiritually awakened, they were open to the next step.

Invite

When we see the shining eyes of someone who has been spiritually awakened, it is time to invite that person into trust-filled relationships with a few other disciples. In our "enterprise" mode of church, we try to shuttle dozens, hundreds, or thousands of people through a one-size-fits-all process to make a disciple.

Although there is value in providing a series of classes to lay out foundational beliefs and practices for living as a disciple, Jesus modeled a crucial truth: we cannot disciple people from a distance. Transformation happens up close.

Jesus invited twelve guys to apprentice with him. Along the way, he taught them, prayed with them, and showed them how to do ministry. But mostly, he spent time with them, a lot of it. They lived, ate, and traveled together 24/7 for three years. This is where the real transformation happened.

In the original Greek of the New Testament, the word for "spend time" is *diatribo*. It's a conjunction of *dia*, which means "against," and *tribo*, which means "to rub." The literal translation is "to rub against" or "to rub off." Jesus knew when he spent time with his disciples, he would rub off on them.[13]

When we invite people into trust-filled relationships, we rub off on each other in several ways.

- Vulnerability – Nothing beats real. Simply sharing our honest questions, doubts, victories, and defeats in a confidential relationship helps us get what it is like to walk with Jesus. About his guys' group, Shane said, "I found out the other guys are just people, too—fallen men saved by grace. One hero in the story…Jesus."

---

13. Ibid., p. 115

- Coaching – When we ask each other good questions and rely on the Holy Spirit to reveal a new awareness of truth, it helps us get unstuck.

- Mentoring – Sometimes it is helpful to share life lessons from our experience.

- Prayer – Although our hard won wisdom can certainly be helpful in someone else's life, what truly brings change on a deep level is prayer. It's the most caring thing we can do for one another.

- Relationship – Discipleship depends on trust and trust is the fruit of friendship. Jesus said to his disciples, "I have called you friends, for everything that I learned from my Father I have made known to you" (John 15:15). Every deep discipleship relationship is a friendship.

As we get to know people on a deeper level, it leads us to…

Visualize

From experience, we know God has been at work in this person's life long before we ever showed up. However, all of us suffer from the same eye disease: spiritual myopia. We are so close to ourselves we often cannot see how God is working our lives.

A crucial role in a discipling relationship is to visualize what God is doing beneath the surface in someone's life. This is not the result of guesswork but of prayer work. If we ask, God will reveal this deeper purpose to us over time.

In essence, we are doing the work of a prophet: we see in others what they don't yet see in themselves and call it out.

It's been called an ICNU conversation for short. Some of us know how life altering it is when someone we trust looks us in the eye and says, "*I see in you* a new thing God is doing."

Reflecting on his small group, a man said, "One of the guys called out something in me during that time that I didn't see or perhaps, more accurately, didn't want to see: a calling into ministry. I know it was Holy Spirit led because now I cannot imagine not doing it."

Once the work of God has been visualized and called out, it's time to…

129

Encourage

The word comes from the old French word *encoragier*, meaning "make strong, hearten," and it may be the most important thing we can do for someone who feels a little queasy about a new step of faith.

Encouragement is oxygen for the soul. We often inspire hope and confidence simply by exuding confidence in someone before he or she can believe it personally.

Another form of encouragement is placing someone in a challenging (but not impossible) position to use his or her gifts and deepen a sense of calling. In these situations, we must be ready to mentor the person when the going gets tough.

Here's the benefit: joy! A woman recently shared that her current church is the first one to truly use her spiritual gifts to further Jesus' mission, instead of asking her to fill an open spot for serving. It's made a life-changing difference for everyone!

As encouragement strengthens a disciple's confidence and ability, the time comes to…

Release

The ultimate goal for a new disciple is to release him or her to go and make other disciples. In fact, that is the acid test. If the person we have discipled does not make other disciples, we have not completed the task. This is the multiplication factor inherent in true disciple-making.

In Paul's second letter to his "son in the gospel," Timothy, he says,

And the things you have heard me say in the presence of many witnesses entrust to reliable people who will also be qualified to teach others.

—2 Timothy 2:2

Let's trace the number of "faith generations" represented here. Paul (first) is encouraging Timothy (second) to entrust to reliable people (third) who will be qualified to teach others (fourth). Imagine how rapidly your small group, Sunday school class, or congregation would grow if everyone involved would make one disciple, who would make another disciple, who would then make another disciple. When we jump in the RIVER, we don't just add. We multiply.

To see this approach in action, let's pick up the "in between" stories of Mike, Chantel, and Shane.

How did Mike go from a jaded church dropout to an ordained pastor influencing hundreds of churches? In one sense, God caught him off guard. He didn't know the impact of practical biblical teaching or how much he needed the authentic relationships in his small group.

But beyond these factors, Mike's secret ingredient was finding a spiritual mentor and becoming friends. Mike says, "I remember one of the first lunches we had together when my mentor asked, 'How is it with your soul today?' I was dumbfounded and had no answer. At first, I thought it was a trick question, but I realized after spending more time together that he really wanted to know how I was doing. He genuinely cared about me, my marriage, my family, and our wellbeing. He cared about my relationship with God. Nobody had shown me that level of deep soul care in my life."

Although Chantel grew up in church, she never really got it. In her early 30s, she heard something about God's grace that touched her deeply and started her on a search. It first led her to people who were unexplainably happy as they served. Not long after, she found a few people at her church who took the time to listen to her and explain simple ways to live out her faith.

She said, "I used to think you were born with spirituality, and I just didn't have it. What I learned was it is an active daily journey that is never just a straight, upward climb. They gave me a framework that changed everything. I will never forget the day I realized I was content. It was something I never thought I would achieve."

As for Shane, he discovered what many high achievers feel: an odd mix of outer success and inner searching. Although he appreciated the large group worship and teaching, he needed a small group for discipleship to become personal.

He said, "The idea of a covenant group was new to me. I needed and wanted it. I craved to go deeper, and the two other guys in my group discipled me in that framework. They were vulnerable about struggles in their lives, which helped me be open about mine. God's holy love increased in my life in that accountability setting. In fact, I have had a group like that running for six years now. It has grown to eight to ten guys and is running itself now. I'm going to launch one in another town this year."

Mike, Chantel, and Shane all experienced people who *relayed* God's word and God's power to them on a personal level. Each of them was *invited* into an up-close relationship where people they trusted *visualized* what God was doing in them. In each case, Mike, Chantel, and Shane were *encouraged* to take bold, new steps of faith. Ultimately, they were *released* to repeat this pattern with others.

Mike summed it up this way: "Discipleship is not just sermons and Bible studies. They are important, but we can consume all the information possible and that alone won't really allow us to go deeper with God or with others. For me, discipleship transformed my life because someone further down the road became my friend and showed me what God's love looks like."

Isn't that what we all need to go deeper? It's in *diatribo* relationships that Jesus can rub off on us and transform our lives.

When something stirs in a person's heart and he or she starts searching for more, let's not settle for offering a consumer-based faith that entertains the mind without transforming the heart. We are dealing with eternal souls. The stakes are too high and the mission too great to offer people a life beneath their privilege in Christ. Instead of inviting people to hang out at the lake and play, let's invite them to jump in the RIVER. There an ever-flowing current brings life to everything it touches.

Join The Revolution

You can't go back and change the beginning,
but you can start where you are and change the ending.

—C. S. Lewis

It came in a text thread.

A pastor shared a revelation that took her by surprise.

I received a leadership assessment from someone we're considering for our Leadership Team. It was pretty shallow. Wondering if there was more, I decided to ask him what spiritual practices he did. He had a hard time answering. This is a man who has been in the church all his life. He is a good person, displays servanthood in many ways, financially generous, and yet, he couldn't answer. It made me sad. And I've been his pastor for a long time...

If our goal is to make church members, my friend's sadness makes no sense. This man has been attending church, serving, and giving his whole life. One can assume he holds certain beliefs about God and Jesus that align with historic Christianity. For decades, he has helped maintain the institution of the church in crucial ways.

Yet, he could not name a single spiritual practice that revealed a personal walk with Jesus—not prayer or Bible engagement, faith sharing or group life, solitude or ministry with the poor. He's solidly in the church, but he doesn't seem to be pursuing a life-giving relationship with Christ or helping others do the same. Something is missing. He's a good church member, but he shows no signs of being a deeply devoted disciple.

He's not alone.

Spiritual writer John Mark Comer notes that around 63 percent of Americans identify as Christians. However, several surveys peg the number of Americans who could be called deeply devoted disciples at about 4 percent.[1]

Perhaps we are missing the core issue. When Jesus appeared to his disciples after his resurrection, he didn't say, "Go, therefore, and make Christians of all nations." He was very specific. He commissioned his disciples to *make disciples* (Matthew 28:19).

In fact, the word "Christian" didn't appear until years later. It literally means "little Christ" and was used to mock early Christ followers by opponents to the faith. Over time, our spiritual forebearers embraced the name to reflect their desire to become like Christ in thought, word, and deed.[2]

Sadly, the word communicates something quite different today. Remember our friend, Lauren, from the Introduction? Her early view of faith had little to do with pursuing a life-altering relationship with Jesus. Like many shaped by Western culture, she thought a Christian simply held a few beliefs about God and Jesus and attended church off and on, if at all.

Contrast that to what the beloved disciple John wrote to the early church: "Whoever claims to live in him must live as Jesus did".[3]

Clearly, there's a disconnect. But even in a highly secular, me-focused culture, God still has a way of entering our distracted lives and flipping the script. A pastor friend shared a recent example.

Jason began attending church about a year before he went to prison. Due to his offense, he had lost everything—his family, his business, his house—and had to move in with his mom. Jason's mom has been a member for many years at the church where my friend serves.

Not only did Jason attend worship with his mom, but he also began attending his mom's Sunday school class that met after the 8:30am service. After his conviction, this group continued to pray for him and wrote letters to him in prison once or twice a month for five years.

One night, alone in his cell, Jason realized how wrong his life had been and how everything he had done on his own had been destructive. In desperation, he cried out, "Please God, I need you more now than ever! I want to come home, but I don't know the way."

---

1. Comer, John Mark, *Practicing the Way: Be with Jesus, Become Like Him, Do as He Did*, Water-Brook, 2024.

2. Ibid.

3. 1 John 2:6

At that very moment, he felt a Presence in his cell, right on his bunk. Jason said,

> *"I can remember hearing in my ears,* **'Believe in me. Believe.'**
>
> *Later, as I thought about it, I realized God was just waiting for me to call on him. God didn't say, 'You have to get to me in heaven.' He didn't say, 'I'll meet you halfway.' God came all the way down to Charlie 18 in 9 House to be with me that night."*

After serving his time, Jason came back to church a different man. His pastor said, "Before prison, Jason was a very bitter person. But now, he is a Spirit-filled and Spirit-led man deeply passionate about his walk with Jesus."

As part of his new life, Jason now co-leads the Sunday school class that exchanged letters with him during his imprisonment. He serves there because that's where he first experienced Jesus' love with skin on.

Jason is quite literally a trophy of God's grace. His life serves as a testimony to how the Holy Spirit can transform any of us through the G's. Jason had no idea when he called out in desperation one night that the very presence of God would show up in his prison cell. In a palpable encounter with God's presence, he experienced God's glory.

But he first tasted grace through his group. Their prayers, their letters, and their support when he felt as though he least deserved it mirrored the unmerited love of God. They simply loved Jason and refused to give up on him.

Both in his group and in various worship experiences, Jason was introduced to Scriptural truth and began to grow as a deeply devoted disciple. As part of his growth, he discovered his giftedness and soon deployed his gifts as a co-leader of his class.

Along the way, God used Jason's own troubled journey to give him a heart of compassion for others who struggle. As a result, his life is now characterized by generosity as he joyfully gives his time and resources to bring Christ's healing, justice, and hope to people in need.

In a word, this is transformation. It is the essence of God's desire for each of our lives and the mission to which Jesus calls every disciple.

Imagine for a moment that receiving and relaying this kind of transformation was the burning passion of every self-identified Christian. Picture the number of lives changed, marriages reconciled, families restored, people healed, and communities thriving. Now pull back for the wide angle. Imagine millions of children saved from abuse, races reconciled, human trafficking stopped, crime rates plummeting, and the poor lifted up with dignity. Take it back one more notch. Envision the end of world hunger, killer diseases like malaria eradicated, a reversal of climate change, and peace breaking out instead of war among nations all over the world.

Recent estimates put the number of Christians in the world at 2.3 billion. What if every one of them became a deeply devoted disciple? Truly, our world would become a radically different place.

Philosopher and spiritual writer, Dallas Willard, says it well:

> *The greatest issue facing the world today, with all its heartbreaking needs, is whether those who ... are identified as "Christians" will become disciples— students, apprentices, practitioners of Jesus Christ, steadily learning from him how to live the life of the Kingdom of the Heavens into every corner of human existence.*[4]

If this were to happen, and God knows it could, it would be a revolution. Let's join it today.

---

4.   Willard, Dallas, *The Great Omission: Reclaiming Jesus's Essential Teachings on Discipleship*, New York, NY: HarperOne, an imprint of HarperCollinsPublishers, 2014.

Acknowledgments

Sometimes God sneaks up on us. In countless conversations with pastors, lay leaders, seminary students, and network leaders, the same subject kept coming up: making church members isn't working. How can we get better at making disciples?

As we batted around ideas, I would mention my previous church's approach to making deeply devoted disciples and rattle off the six G's. Invariably, someone would say, "What was that fourth G again? And do you have this written down anywhere?" That happened so many times, I finally got the hint.

When I brought up the topic with Len Wilson from Invite Ministries, he said, "I've been waiting for two years for someone to propose a book on discipleship." He immediately set the project in motion.

From the beginning, it has been a team effort. I'm indebted to my friends and fellow pastors, Bob Swickard and Mike Whitaker. Together we wrestled with God for many months to discern our three core characteristics and six G's.[5] When we finally revealed them to the leaders of First United Methodist Church of Springfield, Illinois, they gave insightful feedback and enthusiastically endorsed them as the new discipleship process for our church. Now, years later, several hundred people have been through this G6 approach to become deeply devoted disciples.

Shortly after the writing process began, I felt the weight of the project and knew I needed help. Several people became part of the initial prayer team who, like Aaron and Hur, "lifted my arms" so the battle would not be lost. They include Patty Altstetter, Susan Arnold, Chantel Corrie, Barb Cray,

---

5. In writing this book, I changed the second core characteristic from "Build Community" to "Launch Community."

Jill Chrusciel, Richard Heyduck, Val Johnson, Sharla Jolly, Joe & Beth Koberstein, Tom & Stacey Krawcyzk, Sam & Jane Nichols, Mike Potts, Teresa Pratt, Jim Preisig, Leanne Ross, Zach Ross, Sherry Struck, Angela Vincent, and Ervin & Marilyn Williams. Apart from their prayers, this work never would have been completed.

Other gifts of grace came from friends and colleagues who were willing to read initial drafts and give valuable feedback. They include Jorge Acevedo, Andy Adams, Patty Altstetter, Susan Arnold, Ken Cuffey, Matthew Esquivel, Richard Heyduck, Jeff Miller and his Christian Writing Group, Jane Nichols, Donna Schaad, Larry Stimpert, and Ervin Williams. I am deeply grateful for their sacrifice of time and the wisdom they shared.

Speaking of gifts, out of the blue one day, Pastor Mike Gillen and the congregation of St. Luke's United Methodist Church in St. Louis offered to beta test an earlier draft of this material during Lent and give their feedback. Receiving a congregation's insights at that stage was priceless.

My deep appreciation also extends to the team at Invite Ministries. Len Wilson, Stephen Graham-Ching, and Ariana Weberg brainstormed with me, made excellent edits, and gracefully kept the project moving. Clearly, it took a pretty big team to bring this book to life. However, any errors within it are mine.

Finally, I reserve my deepest gratitude for my wife, Leanne, who patiently endured many nights on her own as I typed away upstairs. Her prayers, constant encouragement, and quiet sacrifices are just some of the beautiful ways the love of Jesus shines through her.

Appendix A

Spiritual Disciplines

For centuries, disciples of Jesus have practiced spiritual disciplines to open their hearts and lives to the transforming grace of God. The disciplines themselves do not change us. They merely place us in a position where the Spirit of God can do the kind of inner surgery necessary to restore our souls.

Although there are many classic disciplines of the Christian faith such as prayer, studying Scripture, fasting, giving, and keeping the Sabbath, there is no widely agreed upon set of spiritual disciplines for all disciples. Below are the disciplines described in four respected books on this topic. There will be overlap as well as uniqueness. Feel free to explore any of these books or specific disciplines as the Spirit leads. Practicing the disciplines is more of an art than a science.

- Barton, Ruth Haley, *Sacred Rhythms: Arranging Our Lives for Spiritual Transformation*, Downers Grove, IL: Intervarsity Press, 2006.

    1. Solitude
    2. Scripture
    3. Prayer
    4. Honoring the Body
    5. Self-Examination
    6. Discernment
    7. Sabbath

- Comer, John Mark, *Practicing the Way: Be with Jesus, Become like him, Do as he did*, Colorado Springs: WaterBrook, 2024.

    1. Sabbath
    2. Solitude
    3. Prayer
    4. Fasting
    5. Scripture
    6. Community
    7. Generosity
    8. Service
    9. Witness

- Foster, Richard, *Celebration of Discipline: The Path to Spiritual Growth*, Revised and Expanded, San Francisco: HarperSanFrancisco, 1998.

    The Inward Disciplines

    1. Meditation
    2. Prayer
    3. Fasting
    4. Study

    The Outward Disciplines

    1. Simplicity
    2. Solitude
    3. Submission
    4. Service

    The Corporate Disciplines

    1. Confession
    2. Worship
    3. Guidance
    4. Celebration

- Willard, Dallas, *The Spirit of The Disciplines: Understanding How God Changes Lives*, New York: Harper & Row, Publishers, 1988.

    Disciplines of Abstinence
    1. Solitude
    2. Silence
    3. Fasting
    4. Frugality
    5. Chastity
    6. Secrecy
    7. Sacrifice

Disciplines of Engagement
    1. Study
    2. Worship
    3. Celebration
    4. Service
    5. Prayer
    6. Fellowship
    7. Confession
    8. Submission

About the Author

A native of Cambridge, Illinois, Roger Ross has served as a pastor in Texas, the British Channel Island of Guernsey, and Illinois. While in Illinois, he led teams that planted two new churches and served for ten years as the lead pastor of Springfield First United Methodist Church. He then served as the Director of Congregational Excellence at the Missouri Conference, leading teams to start new churches and transform existing churches across the state. He has also been a coach with Spiritual Leadership, Inc.

Today, Roger serves as the founder of TheHumilityGroup.org, a coaching organization that equips pastors, faith-based leaders, and their teams to lead grace-shaped lives that transform the world. He also leads a network that brings pastors and leaders together to connect, innovate and thrive.

Roger is the author of three previous books: Meet *The Goodpeople: Wesley's 7 Ways to Share Faith, Come Back: Returning to the Life You Were Made For, and Come Back Participant Guide.*

Now for the best part! Roger is married to Leanne Klein Ross. They live in Bloomington, IL, and God has blessed them with two adult children, a son-in-law, and one adorable grand-dog. For fun, Roger enjoys scuba diving in warm blue water and has a weakness for golf.

SCAN HERE to catch Roger's weekly blog on living and leading like Jesus.

143

SCAN HERE to learn more about
Invite Ministries—created to invite people to a deeper
faith and living relationship with Jesus Christ